VOGUE KNITTING
BAGS
&BACKBACKS

VOGUE KNITTING
BAGS
&BACKPACKS

THE BUTTERICK® PUBLISHING COMPANY
NEW YORK

THE BUTTERICK® PUBLISHING COMPANY
161 Avenue of the Americas
New York, New York 10013

Copyright © 2000 by The Butterick® Publishing Company
All rights reserved including the right of reproduction
in whole or in part in any form.

THE BUTTERICK® PUBLISHING COMPANY and colophon
are registered trademarks of Butterick® Company, Inc.

Manufactured in China

1 3 5 7 9 10 8 6 4 2

Library of Congress Cataloging-in-Publication Data Available

ISBN 1-57389-018-9

First Edition

TABLE OF CONTENTS

INTRODUCTION

If you're like most women, you carry your life in your bag. Keys to the car, the house, the office, papers for the latest project at work, a grocery list, and the all-important organizer that keeps track of the whos, whats, whens, wheres, and whys of your increasingly busy life. Between the demands of work and family who has time (let alone room) to add knitting to the mix?

The truth is little windows of knitting opportunity are waiting around every corner. Every endless minute spent at your child's sporting tournament, held over in an airport lounge, or collapsed in front of the TV is a golden opportunity to slip in a few stitches. Add them up and you have all the time you need to finish a project.

Bags are perfect for knitting on the run. Most require little shaping and minimal finishing, and can be easily completed without investing a good deal of time, space, or money (many can be completed with odds and ends from your yarn stash). Their small scale makes them ideal for trying out new stitch patterns and techniques or experimenting with color and texture. Indulge your creative side by making one (or two, or ten) and you'll end up with something beautiful and useful for your efforts.

So make room in your tote for yarn and needles, and get ready to **KNIT ON THE GO!**

THE BASICS

Handbags, purses, backpacks, totes or pouches—one thing is for sure, a woman never leaves home without one of them. Whether your bag holds your wallet and a few grooming necessities or acts as a small suitcase, the handbag you choose to carry is probably one of the most important accessories in your wardrobe.

On the following pages you'll find a variety of bags to fit every taste, season, age, and mood—not to mention skill level.

You'll find a wide assortment of shapes and sizes suitable for everything from a trip to the beach to a night on the town. Many of the larger totes can double as wonderful knitting bags—a unique way to carry around your on-the-go projects.

STRUCTURE OF BAGS AND BACKPACKS
Knitting a bag is a simple undertaking. Many of the designs in this collection are based on squares or rectangles—think of it as knitting a large-scale swatch with some finishing. Most have a single- or double-fold flap with a loop and button or tassel-trimmed closure.

Other bags have side gussets to add width to the inside of the bag. In some cases the gussets may continue on to become straps, in others, separate straps are sewn on. There are also several designs with envelope-style flaps with a V- or U-shaped styling.

Some of the bags are styled as pouches with oval or circular bottoms and straight sides. The circular bottoms are knit from the center outward on double pointed needles or picked up from the sides of the bag and worked inward to the center. The pouch tops are gathered with either an inner drawstring casing or outside eyelets; some have double side-pull drawstrings for easy closure.

Several of the bags are finished with purchased ready-made plastic or wooden handles, and trimmed with beads and mirrors, or appliques for handy usage or decoration. The Textured Woven Bag on page 87 features a unique circular handle that extends from the main body of the bag.

There are also a few backpacks in this book (some with gradated side gussets) with two-strap shoulder styling. One of them, the Chain-link Backpack on page 78, has a nifty back carry or hanging loop, just like the traditional fabric backpack styling.

BAG FABRIC
Unlike most other knitting projects, bags require a firm fabric. This can be accomplished by working in a tighter gauge than average for the particular yarn. To achieve a tighter gauge, knit with needles that are two or three sizes smaller than is recommended on the ball band.

Another method is to felt the knitted bag, as we have done with several of our

GAUGE

Most bag patterns don't rely on a perfect fit as a garment would, but it is still important to knit a gauge swatch. If the gauge is incorrect, a colorwork pattern may become distorted. The type of needles used—straight or circular, wood or metal—will influence gauge, so knit your swatch with the needles you plan to use for the project. Measure gauge as illustrated here. (Launder and block your gauge swatch before taking measurements). Try different needle sizes until your sample measures the required number of stitches and rows. To get fewer stitches to the inch/cm, use larger needles; to get more stitches to the inch/cm, use smaller needles. It's a good idea to keep your gauge swatch in order to test any embroidery, embellishment, blocking, or cleaning methods.

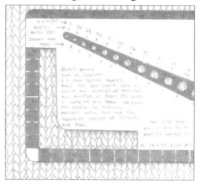

bags, such as the Felted Tote on page 38. The combination of hot water and agitation from the washing machine solidifies the fabric, and gives added structure. Knitted handles can be worked as a double-fabric for sturdy support, as we did in our Felted Sack on page 35.

YARN SELECTION

For an exact reproduction of the bag photographed, use the yarn listed in the Materials section of the pattern. We've selected yarns that are readily available in the U.S. and Canada at the time of printing. The Resources list on page 94 provides addresses of yarn distributors. Contact them for the name of a retailer in your area.

YARN SUBSTITUTION

You may wish to substitute yarns. Perhaps you have a spectacular yarn you've been dying to try, maybe you view small-scale projects as a chance to incorporate leftovers from your yarn stash, or the yarn specified may not be available in your area. Bags allow you to be creative, but you'll need to knit to the given gauge to obtain the knitted measurements with the substitute yarn (see Gauge above). Make pattern adjustments where necessary. Be sure to consider how different yarn types (chenille, mohair, bouclé, etc.) will affect the final appearance of your bag.

Some of the most common fibers used for bags are acrylics or blends for washability, rayon or rayon blends for durability and strength. If you plan to felt your bag it is best to use a yarn that is 100% wool or wool blended with alpaca, mohair or cashmere.

To facilitate yarn substitution, Vogue Knitting grades yarn by the standard stitch gauge obtained in stockinette stitch. You'll find a grading number in the Materials section of the pattern, immediately following the fiber type of the yarn. Look for a substitute yarn that falls into the same category. The suggested needle size and gauge on the ball band should be comparable to that on the Yarn Symbols chart below.

After you've successfully gauge-swatched a substitute yarn, you'll need to figure out how much of the substitute yarn the project requires. First, find the total length of the original yarn in the pattern (multiply number of balls by yards/meters per ball). Divide this figure by the new yards/meters per ball (listed on the ball band). Round up to the next whole number. This is the number of balls required to knit your project.

FOLLOWING CHARTS

Charts provide a convenient way to follow colorwork, lace, cable and other stitch patterns at a glance. Vogue Knitting stitch charts utilize the universal knitting language of "symbolcraft." Unless otherwise indicated, read charts from right to left on right side (RS) rows, and from left to right on wrong side (WS) rows, repeating any stitch and row repeats as directed in the pattern. Posting a self-adhesive note under your working row is an easy way to keep track of your place on a chart.

YARN SYMBOLS

① **Fine Weight**
(29-32 stitches per 4"/10cm)
Includes baby and fingering yarns, and some of the heavier crochet cottons. The range of needle sizes is 0-4 (2-3.5mm).

② **Lightweight**
(25-28 stitches per 4"/10cm)
Includes sport yarn, sock yarn, UK 4-ply and lightweight DK yarns. The range of needle sizes is 3-6 (3-4mm).

③ **Medium Weight**
(21-24 stitches per 4"/10cm)
Includes DK and worsted, the most commonly used knitting yarns. The range of needle sizes is 6-9 (4-5.5mm).

④ **Medium-heavy Weight**
(17-20 stitches per 4"/10cm)
Also called heavy worsted or Aran. The range of needle sizes is 8-10 (5-6mm).

⑤ **Bulky Weight**
(13-16 stitches per 4"/10cm)
Also called chunky. Includes heavier Icelandic yarns. The range of needle sizes is 10-11 (6-8mm).

⑥ **Extra-bulky Weight**
(9-12 stitches per 4"/10cm)
The heaviest yarns available. The range of needle sizes is 11 and up (8mm and up).

COLORWORK KNITTING

Two main types of colorwork are explored in this book.

Intarsia

Intarsia is accomplished with separate bobbins of individual colors. This method is ideal for large blocks of color or for motifs that aren't repeated close together. When changing colors, always pick up the new color and wrap it around the old color to prevent holes.

Stranding

When motifs are closely placed, colorwork is accomplished by stranding along two or more colors per row, creating "floats" on the wrong side of the fabric. When using this method, twist yarns on WS to prevent holes and strand loosely to keep knitting from puckering.

Note that yarn amounts have been calculated for the colorwork method suggested in the pattern. Knitting a stranded pattern with intarsia bobbins will take less yarn, while stranding an intarsia pattern will require more yarn.

BLOCKING

Blocking is the best way to shape pattern pieces and smooth knitted edges. However, some yarns, such as chenilles and ribbons, do not benefit from blocking. Choose a blocking method using information on the yarn care label and, when in doubt, test-block your gauge swatch.

Wet Block Method

Using rust-proof pins, pin the finished bag to measurements on a flat surface and lightly dampen using a spray bottle. Allow to dry before removing the pins.

Steam Block Method

Pin the finished bag to measurements with the wrong side of the knitting facing up. Steam lightly, holding the iron 2"/5cm above the work. Do not press the iron onto the knitting as it will flatten the stitches. This is the better method to use for bags knit in one piece. If you cannot pin the bag flat, simply steam it on the end of an ironing board.

ASSEMBLY

Most bags are knit in one piece. Some are made circularly, therefore no seaming is required. Some are made in squares or rectangles, then folded in half with side seams. Some bags have a separate gusset that is sewn between the front and back pieces.

Seaming can be done using any of these methods:

1. Sewing, using the traditional seaming method used for sweaters.

2. Sewing from the right side, leaving one or two edge stitches free for a decorative ridge, as seen in our Cabled Backpack on page 53.

3. Crocheting, using either slip stitch or single crochet.

4. Embroidery after seaming, using a decorative stitch such as cross stitch or herringbone, as we did in our Felted Tote on page 38.

WORKING A YARN OVER

There are different ways to make a yarn over. Which method to use depends on where you are in the stitch pattern. If you do not make the yarn over in the right way, you may lose it on the following row, or make a yarn over that is too big. Here are the different variations:

Between two knit stitches: Bring the yarn from the back of the work to the front between the two needles. Knit the next stitch, bringing the yarn to the back over the right-hand needle, as shown.

Between a knit and a purl stitch: Bring the yarn from the back to the front between two needles. Then bring it to the back over the right-hand needle and back to the front again, as shown. Purl the next stitch.

Between a purl and a knit stitch: Leave the yarn at the front of the work. Knit the next stitch, bringing the yarn to the back over the right-hand needle, as shown.

Between two purl stitches: Leave the yarn at the front of the work. Bring the yarn to the back over the right-hand needle and to the front again, as shown. Purl the next stitch.

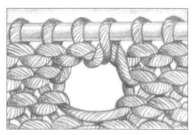

Multiple yarn overs (two or more): Wrap the yarn around the needle, as when working a single yarn over, then continue wrapping the yarn around the needle as many times as indicated. Work the next stitch of the left-hand needle. On the following row, work stitches into the extra yarn overs as described in the pattern. The illustration at right depicts a finished yarn-over on the purl side.

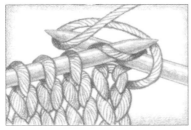

At the beginning of a knit row: Insert the right-hand needle knitwise into the first stitch on the left-hand needle, keeping the yarn in front of the needle. Bring the yarn over the right-hand needle to the back and knit the first stitch, holding the yarn over with your thumb if necessary.

At the beginning of a purl row: Insert the right-hand needle purlwise into the first stitch on the left-hand needle, keeping the yarn behind the needle. Purl the first stitch.

LINING

Adding a fabric lining to your bag has several advantages. It hides the sometimes unfinished look of the "wrong side" of the knitting, adds strength, and can create an interesting design element. The best fabrics to use are washable woven fabrics such as broadcloth, silk or felt. Use the knitted bag as a template to cut out the fabric, adding a ½"/1.25cm seam allowance on all sides. Sew the pieces together as you did for the knitted pieces. With wrong sides together, place the sewn fabric inside the knitted band, turn down the top edge and slip stitch it in place.

CARE

Refer to the yarn label for the recommended cleaning method. Many of the bags in the book can be either washed by hand, or in the machine on a gentle or wool cycle, in lukewarm water with a mild detergent. Do not agitate, and don't soak for more than 10 minutes. Rinse gently with tepid water, then fold in a towel and gently press the water out. Lay flat to dry away from excess heat and light. Check the yarn band for any specific care instructions such as dry cleaning or tumble drying.

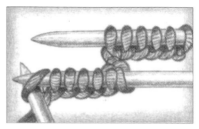

Hold the needle tip with the last cast-on stitch in your right hand and the tip with the first cast-on stitch in your left hand. Knit the first cast-on stitch, pulling the yarn tight to avoid a gap.

1 Cast on the required number of stitches on the first needle, plus one extra. Slip this extra stitch to the next needle as shown. Continue in this way, casting on the required number of stitches on the last needle.

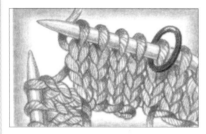

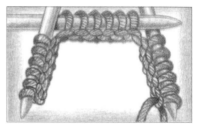

Work until you reach the marker. This completes the first round. Slip the marker to the right needle and work the next round.

2 Arrange the needles as shown, with the cast-on edge facing the center of the triangle (or square).

TWISTED CORD

1 If you have someone to help you, insert a pencil or knitting needle through each end of the strands. If not, place one end over a doorknob and put a pencil through the other end. Turn the strands clockwise until they are tightly twisted.

2 Keeping the strands taut, fold the piece in half. Remove the pencils and allow the cords to twist onto themselves.

3 Place a stitch marker after the last cast-on stitch. With the free needle, knit the first cast-on stitch, pulling the yarn tightly. Continue knitting in rounds, slipping the marker before beginning each round.

THE KITCHENER STITCH

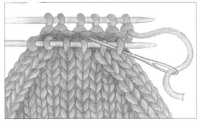

1 Insert tapestry needle purlwise (as shown) through first stitch on front needle. Pull yarn through, leaving that stitch on knitting needle.

2 Insert tapestry needle knitwise (as shown) through first stitch on back needle. Pull yarn through, leaving stitch on knitting needle.

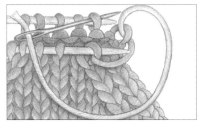

3 Insert tapestry needle knitwise through first stitch on front needle, slip stitch off needle and insert tapestry needle purlwise (as shown) through next stitch on front needle. Pull yarn through, leaving this stitch on needle.

4 Insert tapestry needle purlwise through first stitch on back needle. Slip stitch off needle and insert tapestry needle knitwise (as shown) through next stitch on back needle. Pull yarn through, leaving this stitch on needle.
Repeat steps 3 and 4 until all stitches on both front and back needles have been grafted. Fasten off and weave in end.

DUPLICATE STITCH
Duplicate stitch covers a knit stitch. Bring the needle up below the stitch to be worked. Insert the needle under both loops one row above and pull it through. Insert it back into the stitch below and through the center of the next stitch in one motion, as shown.

KNITTING TERMS AND ABBREVIATIONS

approx approximately

beg begin(ning)

bind off Used to finish an edge and keep stitches from unraveling. Lift the first stitch over the second, the second over the third, etc. (UK: cast off)

cast on A foundation row of stitches placed on the needle in order to begin knitting.

CC contrast color

ch chain(s)

cm centimeter(s)

cn cable needle

cont continu(e)(ing)

dec decrease(ing)—Reduce the stitches in a row (knit 2 together).

dpn double pointed needle(s)

foll follow(s)(ing)

g gram(s)

garter stitch Knit every row. Circular knitting: knit one round, then purl one round.

inc increase(ing)—Add stitches in a row (knit into the front and back of a stitch).

k knit

k2tog knit 2 stitches together

LH left-hand

lp(s) loops(s)

m meter(s)

M1 make one stitch—With the needle tip, lift the strand between last stitch worked and next stitch on the left-hand needle and knit into the back of it. One stitch has been added.

M1 p-st With the needle tip, lift the strand between last stitch worked and next stitch on the left hand needle and purl it. One purl stitch has been added.

MC main color

mm millimeter(s)

no stitch On some charts, "no stitch" is indicated with shaded spaces where stitches have been decreased or not yet made. In such cases, work the stitches of the chart, skipping over the "no stitch" spaces.

oz ounce(s)

p purl

p2tog purl 2 stitches together

pat(s) pattern

pick up and knit (purl) Knit (or purl) into the loops along an edge.

pm place marker(s)—Place or attach a loop of contrast yarn or purchased stitch marker as indicated.

psso pass slip stitch(es) over

rem remain(s)(ing)

rep repeat

rev St st reverse Stockinette stitch-Purl right-side rows, knit wrong-side rows. Circular knitting: purl all rounds. (UK: reverse stocking stitch)

rnd(s) round(s)

RH right-hand

RS right side(s)

sc single crochet (UK: dc—double crochet)

sk skip

SKP Slip 1, knit 1, pass slip stitch over knit 1. One stitch has been decreased.

SK2P Slip 1, knit 2 together, pass slip stitch over the knit 2 together. Two stitches have been decreased.

sl slip-An unworked stitch made by passing a stitch from the left-hand to the right-hand needle as if to purl.

sl st slip stitch (UK: sc—single crochet)

ssk slip, slip, knit—Slip next 2 stitches knitwise, one at a time, to right-hand needle. Insert tip of left-hand needle into fronts of these stitches from left to right. Knit them together. One stitch has been decreased.

sssk Slip next 3 sts knitwise, one at a time, to right-hand needle. Insert tip of left-hand needle into fronts of these stitches from left to right. Knit them together. Two stitches have been decreased.

st(s) stitch(es)

St st Stockinette stitch Knit right-side rows, purl wrong-side rows. Circular knitting: knit all rounds. (UK: stocking stitch)

tbl through back of loop

tog together

WS wrong side(s)

wyib with yarn in back

wyif with yarn in front

work even Continue in pattern without increasing or decreasing. (UK: work straight)

yd yard(s)

yo yarn over-Make a new stitch by wrapping the yarn over the right-hand needle. (UK: yfwd, yon, yrn)

* = repeat directions following * as many times as indicated.

[ ] = Repeat directions inside brackets as many times as indicated.

CROCHET STITCHES

CHAIN

I *Pass the yarn over the hook and catch it with the hook.*

2 *Draw the yarn through the loop on the hook.*

3 *Repeat steps 1 and 2 to make a chain.*

SINGLE CROCHET

I *Insert the hook through top two loops of a stitch. Pass the yarn over the hook and draw up a loop—two loops on hook.*

2 *Pass the yarn over the hook and draw through both loops on hook.*

3 *Continue in the same way, inserting the hook into each stitch.*

CABLED MINI BAG

Twist and shout!

Cable ready? Try out this simple crossover technique. A basic rectangle shape and button-loop closure makes for quick and easy finishing. Designed by Chris Lipert.

KNITTED MEASUREMENTS
- Approx 8"/20.5cm square

MATERIALS
- 1 5oz/140g balls (each approx 275yd/247m) of Bernat *Aspen* (acrylic/wool ④) in #4911 blue
- One pair size 10½ (7mm) needles *or size to obtain gauge*
- Two size 10½ (7mm) dpn
- One 1"/25mm button
- Cable needle

GAUGE
12 sts and 20 rows to 4"/10cm over St st using double strand of yarn and size 10½ (7mm) needles.
Take time to check gauge.

BAG
With double strand of yarn, beg at top edge of bag, cast on 32 sts.

Row 1 (RS) Purl.
Row 2 and all even rows P10, k1, p10, k1, p10.
Row 3 K10, p1, k10, p1, k10.
Rows 5, 7 and 9 Rep row 3.
Row 11 K10, p1, sl 5 sts to cn and hold to back, k5, k5 from cn, p1, k10.
Rows 13 and 15 Rep row 3.
Row 16 Rep row 2.
Rep rows 1-16 for pat 3 times more. Work rows 1-8 once. Bind off purlwise on RS.

FINISHING
Block bag to measurements. Fold bag in half and sew side seams.
Buttonloop
Make a 3"/7.5cm buttonloop by braiding 3 strands of yarn tog. Sew to inside of back. Sew on button at front opposite loop.
I-cord strap
With 2 dpn, cast on 3 sts.
*Next row (RS) K3, do *not* turn. Slide sts to beg of needle to work next row from RS; rep from * until I-cord measures 42"/106cm. Bind off. Sew I-cord to inside edges of bag.

EASY STRIPED BAG
Flip flap

Cool garter-stitch bag with sassy stripes is a great project for the beginning knitter. A simple folded rectangle and easy I-cord strap make for quick construction. Designed by Veronica Manno.

KNITTED MEASUREMENTS

■ Approx 11" x 9½"/28cm x 24cm

MATERIALS

■ 2 1¾oz/50g balls (each approx 160yd/145m) of Garnstudio/Aurora Yarns *Angora-Tweed* (wool/angora ③) each in #09 gold (A), #08 rust (B) and #04 lt green (C)

■ One pair size 8 (5mm) needles *or size to obtain gauge*

■ Two size 8 (5mm) dpn

■ 1½"/38mm toggle button

GAUGE

20 sts and 28 rows to 4"/10cm over garter st using size 8 (5mm) needles.
Take time to check gauge.

STRIPE PATTERN

Working in garter st, work 2 rows A, 2 rows B, 2 rows C. Rep these 6 rows for stripe pat.

BAG

With A, cast 38 sts. Work in stripe pat until piece measures 23"/58.5cm from beg.
Buttonhole row (RS) K17, bind off 4 sts, k to end. On next row, cast on 4 sts over bound-off sts. Cont in stripe pat until piece measures 24"/61cm from beg. Bind off.

FINISHING

Block to measurements. Fold one short end up by 10"/25.5cm. Finish side seams as folded. Flap folds over bag by 3½"/9cm.
I-cord strap
With dpn and A, cast on 4 sts.
***Next row (RS)** K4, do *not* turn. Slide sts to beg of needle to work next row from RS; rep from *until I-cord measures 46"/117cm. Bind off. Sew I-cord to outer side seams of bag, overlapping at edge by 3"/7.5cm.

BASIC BASKETWEAVE
Check mate!

This simple bag is worked in one long rectangle then folded up to finish. Elementary stitch patterning provides a stepping stone for new knitters ready to tackle the next step.

KNITTED MEASUREMENTS

▪ Approx 10½" x 9½"/26.5cm x 24cm

MATERIALS

▪ 4 1¾oz/50g balls (each approx 107yd/98m) of Lion Brand *AL•PA•KA* (acrylic/wool/alpaca ③) in #249 grey tweed

▪ One pair size 11 (8mm) needles *or size to obtain gauge*

▪ Two size 10½ (7mm) dpn

GAUGE

10 sts and 15 rows to 4"/10cm over pat st using double strand of yarn and size 11 (8mm) needles.

Take time to check gauge.

BAG

With a double strand of yarn, cast on 28 sts.

Row 1 (RS) K4, *p4, k4; rep from * to end.

Row 2 P4, *k4, p4; rep from * to end.

Rows 3 and 4 Rep rows 1 and 2.

Row 5 Rep row 2.

Row 6 Rep row 1.

Rows 7 and 8 Rep rows 5 and 6.

Rep rows 1-8 for pat st until piece measures 28"/71cm from beg. Bind off in pat.

FINISHING

Block to measurements. Fold one short end up by 10"/25.5cm. Finish side seams as folded. Flap folds over bag by 7"/18cm.

I-cord strap

With double strand of yarn and dpn, cast on 4 sts.

***Next row (RS)** K4, do *not* turn. Slide sts to beg of needle to work next row from RS; rep from * until I-cord measures 38"/96.5cm. Bind off. Sew I-cord to outer side seams of bag, overlapping on edge by 2"/5cm.

FRINGED MINI BAG

Take a ribbing

Very Easy Very Vogue

Two super-simple ribbed rectangles make up this handy little shoulder bag. Finished with an easy I-cord strap and knotted fringe, it's a perfect first project. Designed by Daryl Brower.

KNITTED MEASUREMENTS

- Approx 8" x 5½"/20.5cm x 14cm

MATERIALS

- 1 7½oz/250g skein (each approx 310yd/286m) of Wool Pak Yarns NZ/Baabajoes Wool Co. *14-Ply* (wool ⑤) in teal
- One pair size 15 (10mm) needles *or size to obtain gauge*
- Two size 15 (10mm) dpn
- Size G/6 (4.5mm) crochet hook
- One 1"/25mm button

GAUGE

13 sts and 17 rows to 4"/10cm over k2, p2 rib using size 15 (10mm) needles.
Take time to check gauge.

BACK

Cast on 20 sts.

Row 1 (RS) P1, *k2, p2; rep from *, end k2, p1.

Row 2 K1, *p2, k2; rep from *, end p2, k1.

Rep rows 1 and 2 for k2, p2 rib until piece measures 8½"/21.5cm from beg. Bind off.

FRONT

Work as for back.

FINISHING

Block pieces to measurements. Sew 3 sides tog leaving top open. With crochet hook, ch 22 for buttonloop. Fasten buttonloop firmly at center back. Sew on button 1"/2.5cm down from center front. Cut eight 10"/25.5cm lengths of yarn for each fringe. Attach 5 fringes to lower edge.

I-cord strap

With 2 dpn, cast on 3 sts.

***Next row (RS)** K3, do *not* turn. Slide sts to beg of needle to work next row from RS; rep from * until I-cord measures 34"/86cm. Sew cord to inside top of bag.

CHUNKY TOTE
Downtown basic

Very Easy Very Vogue

This super-sturdy tote, perfect for catering to your daily needs, is super quick to knit in extra-bulky yarn. Finishing is minimal; get a grip with the chic square handles. Designed by Jean Guirguis.

KNITTED MEASUREMENTS
▨ Approx 12" x 13"/30.5cm x 33cm

MATERIALS
▨ 4 6oz/170g balls (each approx 108yd/97m) of Lion Brand *Wool-Ease Thick & Quick* (acrylic/wool ⑥) in #152 pewter
▨ One pair size 17 (12.75mm) needles *or size to obtain gauge*
▨ One pair black 5"/12.5cm square handles by Judi & Co.

GAUGE
7 sts and 10 rows to 4"/10cm using double strand of yarn and size 17 (12.75mm) needles.
Take time to check gauge.

BAG
With double strand of yarn cast on 36 sts.
Row 1 (RS) P1, k10, p1, k12, p1, k10, p1.
Row 2 K1, p10, k1, p12, k1, p10, k1.
Rep rows 1 and 2 for 9½"/24cm more, end with a RS row. P 1 row.
Next row Bind off 11 sts at beg of next 2 rows. Cont in pat as established on 14 sts for 7"/18cm more. P 1 row. Cont in pat as established for 9½"/24cm more. Bind off.

FINISHING
Block to measurements. Foll diagram join the sides of A to B and C to D with seams on WS. Center one handle to outside of bag top and overcast firmly in place. Sew on other handle in same way.

TOTE BAG DIAGRAM

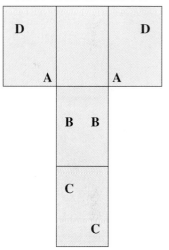

Join the sides of A to B, C to D to complete tote bag

City chic

Stylish shaping and textural embellishments of Lazy Daisy and French knots add up to one chic sac. Easy Stockinette side panels change to ribbing for the straps, the base is worked in reverse. Designed by Teva Durham.

KNITTED MEASUREMENTS

- Approx 13" x 6½"/33cm x 16.5cm

MATERIALS

- 5 1¾oz/50g balls (each approx 66yd/60m) of Trendsetter *Fashion Merino* (wool ③) in #29 red
- One pair size 13 (9mm) needles *or size to obtain gauge*
- Straight pins
- Tapestry needle

GAUGE

10 sts and 12 rows to 4"/10cm over St st with 2 strands held tog and size 13 (9mm) needles.

Take time to check gauge.

BAG

With 2 strands held tog, cast on 28 sts for top of front. Work in St st for 4½"/11.5cm. Work in rev St st for 3"/7.5cm for base of bag. Work in St st for 4½"/11.5cm for back piece, end with a WS row.

Flap

Purl across next RS row (top of purse flap). Cont in St st, AT SAME TIME, when piece measures 14"/35.5cm from beg, dec 1 st each side *every* row 8 times. Bind off rem 12 sts.

SIDES AND STRAP

With 2 strands held tog, cast on 9 sts. Work in St st for 4½"/11.5cm for side piece, AT SAME TIME, dec 1 st each side every 4th row twice—5 sts.

Next row (RS) Beg strap as foll: K1, p1, k1, p1, k1.

Next row K the knit sts and p the purl sts. Cont in rib as established until strap measures 17"/43cm. Work in St st for 4½"/11.5cm for side, AT SAME TIME, inc 1 st each side every 4th row twice. Bind off 9 sts.

FINISHING

With WS facing, fold purse around side pieces and pin in place. With single strand of yarn and tapestry needle, use back st to sew side seams.

With tapestry needle and single strand, using photo as guide, embroider purse flap with lazy daisies and French knots as shown.

FELTED COIN PURSE
Quick change

Luxurious alpaca yarn takes to the felting process beautifully in this charming mini purse. It's uniquely finished with a clever hand closure, braided strap and contrasting embroidered knots. Designed by Linda Niemeyer.

KNITTED MEASUREMENTS

- Approx 8" x 6"/20.5cm x 15cm (after felting)

MATERIALS

- 2 2oz/60g skeins (each approx 120yd/108m) of Blue Sky Alpacas *100% Alpaca Yarn* (alpaca ③) in #100 black (MC)
- 1 skein in #23 red (CC)
- One set (4) size 10½ (7mm) dpn *or size to obtain gauge*
- One 2¼"/60mm novelty hand button by Creative Fibers

GAUGE

12 sts and 20 rnds to 4"/10cm over St st using size 10½ (7mm) dpn before felting. *Take time to check gauge.*

Note Bag is knit in rnds on dpns beg at top edge and ending at lower rounded edge. Flap sts are picked up and knit after bag is worked.

BAG

Beg at top edge, cast on 40 sts. Divide sts evenly on 3 needles. Join, taking care not to twist sts on needle. Mark end of rnd and sl marker every rnd. Work in rnds of St st for 31 rnds.

Dec rnd 1 Ssk, k2tog, k16, ssk, k2tog, k16—36 sts. K 1 rnd.

Dec rnd 2 Ssk, k2tog, k14, ssk, k2tog, k14—32 sts. K 1 rnd.

Dec rnd 3 Ssk, k2tog, k12, ssk, k2tog, k12—28 sts.

Cont to dec 4 sts in this way every rnd, having 2 less sts between double decs, until 6 sts rem. Pull yarn through rem sts and fasten off.

FLAP

Pick up and k 20 sts along one side of cast-on edge so that seam is on inside of bag. Working back and forth in rows with 2 dpn, work in St st for 19 rows.

Top shaping

Dec row 1 (RS) Ssk, k16, k2tog—18 sts. P 1 row, k 1 row.

Dec row 2 P2tog, p14, p2tog—16 sts. K 1 row, p 1 row.

Dec row 3 Ssk, k1, ssk, k1, ssk, k2tog, k1, k2tog, k1, k2tog—10 sts. P 1 row.

Dec row 4 [Ssk] twice, k2, [k2tog] twice. Bind off rem 6 sts.

FINISHING

Refer to page 37 for information on felting. Lay bag flat to dry. Trim fuzz if desired.

Braided cord

Using 3 strands of MC for each section, make a 50"/127cm length braid to attach around outer contours of bag and to form strap. Knot at end and leave ends for tassel. With CC, embroider French knots through center of cord at ½"/1.25cm intervals for the 18"/45.5cm that cord fits to contour of bag. Sew cord in place and knot firmly at tassel end. Attach novelty hand button to flap. Make a 2"/5cm braided strip for closure for hand button. Attach to bag firmly for button and trim ends.

FRENCH KNOT

Draw the needle up through the work, wrap the yarn once or twice around the needle, and hold yarn taut. Reinsert the needle at the closest point to where the yarn emerged, gently pulling it through to the back of the work.

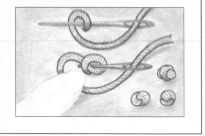

FELTED SACK
Grab bag

This versatile, roomy bag features a gathered drawstring and an extra-sturdy, double-layered shoulder strap. The bag is felted in the washing machine to add extra strength and wearability. Designed by Eileen Mehl.

KNITTED MEASUREMENTS

■ Before felting: 14"/35cm width at base, 14½"/37cm tall, strap is 39"/99cm long by 2½"/6.5cm wide.

■ After felting: 12"/32cm width at base, 16"/40.5cm tall, strap is 35"/89cm long by 2"/5cm wide.

MATERIALS

■ 5 3½oz/100g balls (each approx 110yd/100m) of Tahki Imports *Soho Bulky* (wool ⑤) in #354 blue
■ One size 10 (6mm) circular needle, 36"/92cm long *or size to obtain gauge*
■ One set (4) size 10 (6mm) dpn
■ 4 Tri buttons from K1C2
■ Size I/9 (5.5mm) crochet hook
■ Stitch markers and holder

GAUGES

■ Before felting: 12 sts and 16 rows to 4"/10cm over reverse St st using size 10 (6mm) needles.

■ After felting: 15 sts and 20 rows to 4"/10cm over reverse St st using size 10 (6mm) needles.

Take time to check gauges.

BAG

Beg at base of bag, cast on 38 sts using provisional cast-on method as foll: Using crochet hook and waste yarn in a contrasting color, ch 40. With main yarn and leaving a 10"/25.5cm tail, pick up 38 sts in back ridges of ch. Work in rev St st (p 1 row, k 1 row) for 20 rows.

Beg rnds

Pick up and k 20 sts along side edge of rectangle, pm, unravel waste yarn and pick up and k 38 sts from provisional cast-on edge, pm, pick up and k 20 sts along other side of rectangle, pm—116 sts. The last marker marks beg of rnd. Join and beg working in rnds.

Rnd I Sl marker, M1, p38, M1, sl marker, p20, sl marker, M1, p38, M1, sl marker, p20. P 1 rnd.

Rnd 3 Inc 1 st by M1 after first marker, M1 before 2nd marker, M1 after 3rd marker and M1 before 4th marker. The sts that are inc'd from the front and back of bag and the 20 sts at each side form the shoulder strap. Cont in reverse St st (p every rnd), inc 4 sts as on rnd 3, every other rnd 25 times more—220 sts. Work even until bag measures 16"/40.5cm tall. Bind off 90 sts, p until there are 20 sts from bind-off and sl these sts to a holder, bind off 90 sts.

Beg strap

P5 with first dpn, p10 with 2nd dpn, p5 with 3rd dpn. Join and work in rnds on these sts (the 10 sts on 2nd dpn from the outside of strap) in reverse St st until strap measures 35"/89cm. Sl sts from holder to dpn and weave tog sts from opposite side of bag in the same order (5, 10, 5) as strap sts. Sew open ends of strap tog to close strap at bag top.

FINISHING

Felt bag in washing machine (add heavy towels or old jeans for weight) on normal cycle using hot water and a mild detergent. Rinse in cold water. Lay flat to dry and smooth to a neat shape. Make two 36"/92cm ch cords leaving a 6"/15cm yarn length at each end. Work a sl st in each ch to end. Beg at center, pull cord through fabric, in and out at 4"/10cm intervals at 1"/2.5cm down from bag top. Tie cords tog at center front and back. Attach buttons to 4 cord ends.

Tips on felting

Before knitting your bag, felt your gauge swatch as foll:

Fill washing machine to low water setting at a hot temperature (approximately 100-110°F/40-45°C). Add 1/8 cup of baking soda and 1/4 to 1/2 cup detergent. Add a small towel to provide abrasion and balanced agitation. Use 10-12 minute wash cycle, including cold rinse and spin. Check to see if the approximate gauge has been achieved. If not, then repeat the process with progressively shorter cycles. Check every few minutes until you get the approximate gauge. Record details of water amount, temperatures and cycle lengths.

To felt the finished bag, repeat the above process using the high water setting, a large towel, proportionate amount of detergent (at least 1/4 cup baking soda and 1 cup detergent). Run through 1 normal cycle. Check the bag frequently for signs of felting. Proceed as for the gauge swatch, but note that due to difference in size and weight, the bag may felt much quicker than the swatch.

Check the bag frequently using your swatch as a guide. Remove the bag when you are getting the proper size and texture. Run through the spin cycle to remove excess water. Lie the bag flat to dry on towels, changing to a fresh towel when necessary. Some blocking may be done by patting and stretching.

FELTED TOTE
Folk lure

Eight alternating strips of Fair Isle and stripe patterns play off each other in this roomy tote. Wooden bead handles, blanket stitch, and oversized cross-stitches add to the handcrafted look. Designed by Wendy Sacks.

KNITTED MEASUREMENTS

■ 14½" x 17"/37cm x 43cm (after felting)

MATERIALS

■ 2 1¾oz/50g balls (each approx 108yds/100m) of Dale of Norway *Heilo* (wool ③) each in #0090 black (A), #004 grey (B), #2931 beige (C), and #9335 green (G)

■ 1 ball each in #4137 red (D), #5545 blue (E) and #2537 gold (F)

■ Two size 10½ (7mm) dpn *or size to obtain gauge*

■ Size G/6 (4.5mm) crochet hook

■ One 1¼"/32mm button

■ Purchased 26"/66cm strung wooden bead handles from Trendsetter Yarn

■ Button

■ Stiff bristle brush (for felting)

GAUGES

■ Before felting: 16 sts and 17 rows to 4"/10cm in St st foll charts using size 10½ (7mm) needles before felting.

■ After felting: 18 sts and 21 rows to 4"/10cm.

Take time to check gauges.

Notes 1) Strips are knit back and forth on 2 dpn to make changing colors at either end of row easier. **2)** Bag is made with 4 alternating stripe strips and 4 Fair Isle strips and pieces are sewn tog.

FAIR ISLE STRIP 1

(make 2)

With C, cast on 20 sts. Working in St st foll chart, work rows 1-61 once then rep rows 1-24. Piece measures approx 20"/50.5cm. Bind off.

FAIR ISLE STRIP 2

(make 2)

With C, cast on 20 sts. Working in St st foll chart, work rows 30-61 once then rep rows 1-53. Bind off.

STRIPE STRIP 3

(make 4)

With A, cast on 20 sts. Working in St st foll chart, rep rows 1-24 three times, then work rows 1-13 once. Bind off.

FINISHING

Block pieces flat. Foll strip layout, assemble front and back with seams on the WS. Work a tight second seam on lower edge of bag on WS for extra strength. Do not sew side seams, but run a basting thread along top of bag to keep sts from distorting when felting.

FELTING PROCESS

See page 37 for information on felting. Brush with stiff brush to achieve fuzzy fabric. Fold top 1"/2.5cm down to inside for hem and baste in place. Sew side seams firmly, curving lower corners. Using A, work blanket st around top edge. Using C, D and E, embroider cross sts at strip joinings foll photo. With A, make a 9"/23cm twisted cord and loop through center back and fasten in place for buttonloop. Attach handles to inside top hem at strip joinings. Sew on button.

FAIR ISLE STRIPS 1 & 2

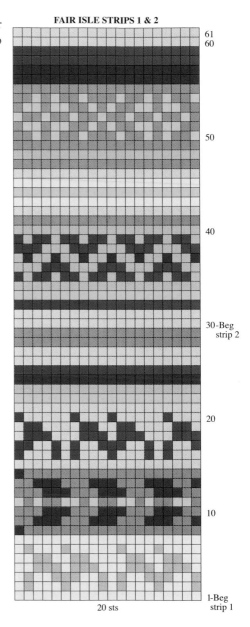

Color key

Black (A)

Grey (B)

Beige (C)

Red (D)

Blue (E)

Gold (F)

Green (G)

STRIPE STRIP 3

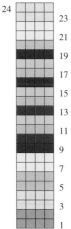

STRIP LAYOUT

| 2 | 3 | 1 | 3 |

20 sts

LEAF APPLIQUÉ HANDBAG

Autumn splendor

For Intermediate Knitters

Ultrasuede® maple leaves and matching crystal beads adorn this ridged handbag with top zipper closure, from the Cleckheaton Design Studio. Rib stitches knit on small needles provide firm structure.

KNITTED MEASUREMENTS
■ Approx 9"/23cm square

MATERIALS
■ 3 1¾oz/50g balls (each approx 110yd/100m) of Cleckheaton *Mohair 12 ply* (mohair/nylon/wool ⑤) in #267 red
■ One pair size 3 (3mm) needles *or size to obtain gauge*
■ Size D/3 (3mm) crochet hook
■ ¼yd/.25m rose ultra suede fabric
■ 2 dozen red crystal beads
■ 7"/18cm zipper

GAUGE
27 sts and 32 rows to 4"/10cm over rib pat using size 3 (3mm) needles.
Take time to check gauge.

BACK
Cast on 55 sts.
Row 1 *K2, p2; rep from * end, k2, p1.
Rep row 1 for rib pat, inc 1 st each side (in pat) *every* row 6 times—67 sts. Work even until piece measures 9½"/24cm from beg, end with a RS row.
Next row (WS) Work in pat, dec 9 sts evenly across—58 sts.
Next row (RS) K8, yo, k2tog, k to last 10 sts, yo, k2tog, k8. Work in St st for 11 rows more (facing). Bind off *loosely.*

FRONT
Work as for back.

STRAPS
(make 2)
With crochet hook, ch 5, join with a sl st to first ch to form ring.
Rnd 1 Ch 1, 1 dc in each ch to end, sl st in top of first ch.
Rnd 2 Ch 1, 1 dc in each dc, sl st in top of ch-1. Rep last rnd until strap measures 12"/30cm. Fasten off.

FINISHING
Block pieces to measurements. Cut out 5 leaves (see template on next page) and glue (or sew) to front of bag foll photo. Sew seed pearls around leaves. Sew in zipper at top of facing. Sew straps to top of bag pulling ends through eyelet holes and secure in place. Sew side seams and lower seam of bag.

Leaf Templates

All the Raj

Indian textiles were the inspiration for this stylish pouch. Knit in rich jewel tones, it's adorned with small circular shisha mirrors and decorative embroidery. Leather lacing provides the closure and the shoulder strap. Designed by Mags Kandis.

KNITTED MEASUREMENTS

- Approx 11" x 9½"/28cm x 24cm

MATERIALS

- 1 1¾oz/50g ball (each approx 85yd/78m) of Mission Falls/Unique Kolours *1824 Wool* (wool ③) each in #004 charcoal (A), #003 oyster (B), #016 thyme (C), #010 russet (D), #021 denim (E), #024 amethyst (F) and #014 dijon (G)
- One pair size 6 (4mm) needles *or size to obtain gauge*
- Size 6 (4mm) circular needle, 16"/40cm long
- Size F/5 (4mm) crochet hook
- Twelve 18mm acrylic "shisha" mirrors
- Leather lacing, 34"/86cm for drawstring and 54"/137cm for shoulder strap

GAUGE

20 sts and 26 rows to 4"/10cm over St st using size 6 (4mm) needles.
Take time to check gauge.

BOTTOM

With F, cast on 19 sts. Foll chart for stripes, inc 1 st each side of every row 10 times—39 sts. Work even for 15 rows. Dec 1 st each side of next row then every row 9 times more—19 sts. Bind off. Place

a yarn marker to mark center bound-off st.

BAG

With circular needle and A, beg and end at center yarn marker, pick up and k 98 sts evenly around outside edge of bottom. Do not join, but turn and work back and forth in rows as foll: k 1 row on WS.

Beg chart 1

Row 1 (RS) Foll row 1 of chart 1, work first st of chart, work 48 sts of rep twice, work last st of chart. Cont to foll chart in this way through row 37. With B, beg with a p row, work even in St st for 13 rows.

Drawstring eyelet row (RS) K2, *k2tog, yo twice, ssk, k6; rep from *, end last rep k2.

Next row *P to double yo, p into front of first yo, p into back of second yo; rep from *, end p3. Cont with B in St st for 2 rows.

Beg chart 2

Row 1 (RS) Foll row 1 of chart 2, work first st of chart, work 48 sts of rep twice, work last st of chart. Cont to foll chart in this way through row 20.

Lining

Cont in St st, work stripe pat as foll: 3 rows C, 3 rows D, 3 rows E, 3 rows G and 3 rows F. Bind off.

FINISHING

Block to measurements.

Embroidery

Using contrast colors as in photo, embroider small French knots in center of each square around top and lower sections of bag. Using contrast colors, work straight sts around drawstring eyelets (see photo).

Crochet rings

Using contrast colors as in photo, work with crochet hook as foll: Ch 8, join to first ch; to form ring. Ch 1, work 12 sc into ring: Secure, leaving a long end for sewing. Sew ring to center of diamond and slip mirror in place before sewing down completely. Fold over stripe lining at top of bag and sew in place. Sew back seam. Pull shorter leather lacing through drawstring eyelets and knot ends. Pull shoulder strap lacing through center back seam at 2 eyelets. Knot ends.

Color key

- Charcoal (A)
- Oyster (B)
- Thyme (C)
- Russet (D)
- Denim (E)
- Amethyst (F)
- Dijon (G)

Chart 1

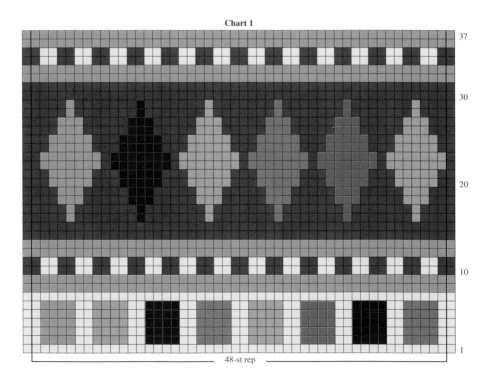

48-st rep

Chart 2

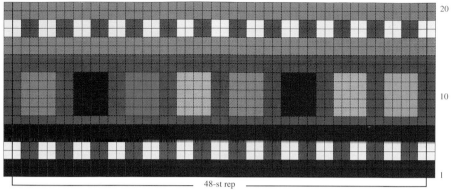

20

10

1

48-st rep

Stripe Chart

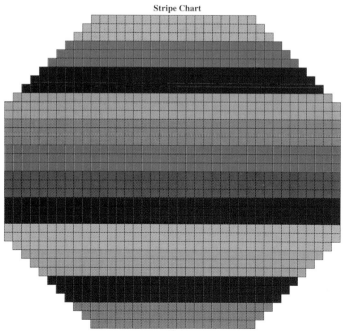

19 sts

DAISY MINI TOTE

Flower power

This clever bag, worked in the round, features a colorfully-striped lining that peeks through eyelet holes to create the daisy centers. Sunburst embroidery through both layers forms the petals. Designed by Védís Jónsdóttir.

KNITTED MEASUREMENTS
▦ Approx 8½" x 8"/21.5cm x 20.5cm

MATERIALS
▦ 2 1¾oz/50g balls (each approx 109yds/100m) of Reynolds/JCA *Lite Lopi* (wool ③) in #5 black heather (MC)
▦ 1 ball each in #441 green (A), #439 red (B), #435 gold (C), #445 teal (D), #436 orange (E) and #54 ash heather (F)
▦ One pair size 5 (3.75mm) needles
▦ One set (5) size 8 (5mm) dpn *or size to obtain gauge*
▦ Tapestry needle

GAUGE
18 sts and 29 rnds to 4"/10cm over St st using size 8 (5mm) dpn.
Take time to check gauge.

Note Bag is knit in rounds using dpn. Contrast cast-on yarn is removed after knitting to graft lower edge sts tog.

BAG
Beg at lower edge with contrast (waste) yarn and dpn, cast on 80 sts. Cut waste yarn and join work, dividing sts evenly on 4 needles. With MC, k 7 rnds.

Rnd 8 *K3, work 2-st eyelet as foll: k2tog, yo twice, ssk, k3; rep from * 7 times more.
Rnd 9 K around, working into each yo as foll: p1 into the first yo, p1 tbl into the second yo.
Rnds 10-18 Knit.
Rnd 19 *Ssk, k6, k2tog, yo twice; rep from * 7 times more.
Rnd 20 Rep rnd 9.
Rnds 21-29 Knit.
Rep rnds 8-29 once more. Rep rnds 8 and 9. K 6 rnds. P 1 rnd (for turning ridge at top). K 3 rnds. Cont in St st only, work striped lining as foll: 9 rnds A, 11 rnds B, 11 rnds C, 11 rnds D, 11 rnds E. With RS facing, divide sts evenly on 2 needles. Using E, graft sts of lining tog. Remove contrast yarn from cast-on edge and graft lower edge tog with MC. Fold lining to inside.

FINISHING
Block lightly to finished measurements. Using F, embroider daisies through both thicknesses using overcast st (see photo). Mark positions for handles at 4 rnds down from turning ridge and leaving 46 sts free at center.

HANDLES
(make 2)
With contrast (waste) yarn, cast on 4 sts with size 5 (3.75mm) needles. Change to MC and work in garter st for 12½"/32cm. Leave sts on a holder. Graft straps to bag at markers.

CABLED CARRY-ALL

Hold everything!

Chunky cables and bobble stitches accent Kirsten Cowan's envelope-style shoulder bag. For sturdiness, the doubled shoulder strap extends from the cabled gusset.

KNITTED MEASUREMENTS
- Approx 12" x 18"/30.5cm x 45.5cm

MATERIALS
- 5 3½oz/100g balls (each approx 223yd/204m) of Patons® *Classic Merino Wool* (wool ③) in #210 pink
- One pair size 11 (8mm) needles *or size to obtain gauge*
- One set (4) size 11 (8mm) dpn
- Cable needle
- One 2"/50mm novelty toggle button

GAUGE
12 sts and 15 rows to 4"/10cm over St st using 2 strands of yarn and size 11 (8mm) needles.
Take time to check gauge.

Note Work with 2 strands of yarn held tog throughout.

STITCH GLOSSARY
4-st LC
Sl 2 sts to cn and hold to *front*, k2, k2 from cn.
4-st RC
Sl 2 sts to cn and hold to *back*, k2, k2 from cn.
3-st LPC
Sl 2 sts to cn and hold to *front*, p1, k2 from cn.

3-st RPC
Sl 1 st to cn and hold to *back* , k2, p1 from cn.
8-st LC
Sl 4 sts to cn and hold to *front*, k4, k4 from cn.
Make Bobble (MB)
Make 5 sts in 1 st by k1 into front, back, front, back and front of st, [turn, p5, turn k5] twice. With LH needle, pull the second, third, fourth and fifth sts one at a time over the first st and off the needle.

CABLE PATTERN
(over 50 sts)
Row 1 (RS) [P2, k4] twice, p3, k2, p4, k8, p4, k2, p3, [k4, p2] twice.
Row 2 [K2, p4] twice, k3, p2, k4, p8, k4, p2, k3, [p4, k2] twice.
Row 3 [P2, 4-st LC] twice, p3, 3-st LPC, p3, k8, p3, 3-st RPC, p3, [4-st RC, p2] twice.
Row 4 [K2, p4] twice, k4, p2, k3, p8, k3, p2, k4, [p4, k2] twice.
Row 5 [P2, k4] twice, p2, MB, p1, 3-st LPC, p2, k8, p2, 3-st RPC, p1, MB, p2, [k4, p2] twice.
Row 6 [K2, p4] twice, k5, p2, k2, p8, k2, p2, k5, [p4, k2] twice.
Row 7 [P2, k4] twice, p4, 3-st RPC, p2, 8-st LC, p2, 3-st LPC, p4, [k4, p2] twice.
Row 8 Rep row 4.
Row 9 [P2, 4-st LC] twice, p3, 3-st RPC, p3, k8, p3, 3-st LPC, p3, [4-st RC, p2] twice.
Row 10 Rep row 2.
Row 11 [P2, k4] twice, p2, 3-st RPC, p1, MB, p2, k8, p2, MB, p1, 3-st LPC, p2, [k4, p2] twice.

Row 12 [K2, p4] twice, k2, p2, k5, p8, k5, p2, k2, [p4, k2] twice.
Row 13 [P2, k4] twice, p2, 3-st LPC, p4, k8, p4, 3-st RPC, p2, [k4, p2] twice.
Rep rows 2-13 for cable pat.

FRONT

With 2 strands of yarn, beg at top edge, cast on 42 sts.
Row 1 (RS) K2, *p2, k2; rep from * to end.
Row 2 P2, *k2, p2; rep from * to end. Rep row 1 once more.
Preparation row (WS) [K2, p2, p into front and back of next st for inc 1-p] twice, k3, inc 1-p, k4, inc 1-p, p4, inc 1-p, k4, inc 1-p, k3, [p2, inc 1-p, k2] twice—50 sts.
Beg cable pat
Work rows 1-13 once, omitting bobbles on rows 5 and 11 (work p1 instead, this is so that bobbles are not protruding when flap is closed), then rep rows 2-13 twice more. Bind off knitwise.

BACK AND FLAP

With 2 strands of yarn, cast on 50 sts. Work rows 1-13 of cable pat, then rep rows 2-13 three times more.
Beg flap
Next row (WS) P2tog, work pat to last 2 sts, p2tog.
Next row (RS) SKP, work pat to last 2 sts, k2tog. Rep these 2 rows 11 times more—2 sts rem. Cut yarn and draw through sts tightly.

STRAP AND GUSSET

Cast on 20 sts.
Rows 1, 3, 5 (RS) P6, k8, p6.
Row 2 and all WS rows K6, p8, k6.
Row 7 P6, 8-st LC, p6.
Rows 9 and 11 P6, k8, p6.
Row 12 K6, p8, k6.
Rep rows 1-12 for 21 times more. Strap measures approx 76"/193cm. Bind off.

FINISHING

Block pieces to measurements. Sew long sides of strap tog forming a tube. Sew cast-on and bound-off edges tog. With cabled edge of strap to outside and center short seam on bottom of bag, sew to outside edges of bag, joining back and front tog for bottom and side gussets. Sew upper (extended) edge of back to inside of strap (to anchor strap in place.)

I-CORD TRIM

With 2 strands of yarn and with dpn, cast on 4 sts.
*Next row (RS) K4, do not turn. Slide sts to beg of needle to work next row from RS; rep from * until I-cord fits along triangular edge of flap plus 2"/5cm extra for buttonloop. Bind off.
Pin I-cord to edge of flap and sew in place leaving the 2"/5cm free at point for buttonloop. Sew button opposite buttonloop.

CABLED BACKPACK
Drawstring dash

This handy backpack with easy-access cord finishing has charm to spare. The cable and bobble pattern, accented with tweedy wool, is surprisingly simple to master. Designed by Norah Gaughan.

KNITTED MEASUREMENTS

- Approx 13½" x 13"/34cm x 33cm

MATERIALS

- 3 3½oz/100g balls (each approx 220yd/203m) of Reynolds/JCA *Turnberry Tweed* (wool ③) in #66 fuchsia
- One pair each sizes 5 and 7 (3.75 and 4.5mm) needles *or size to obtain gauge*
- Two size 5 (3.75mm) dpn
- Cable needle

GAUGE

23 sts and 27 rows to 4"/10cm over cable pat using larger needles.

Take time to check gauge.

STITCH GLOSSARY

4-st RC

Sl 2 sts to cn and hold to *back*, k2, k2 from cn.

4-st LC

Sl 2 sts to cn and hold to *front*, k2, k2 from cn.

4-st RPC

Sl 2 sts to cn and hold to *back*, k2, p2 from cn.

4-st LPC

Sl 2 sts to cn and hold to *front*, p2, k2 from cn.

Make Bobble

K into the front, back,front, back and front

of st to make 5 sts, sl these 5 sts to LH needle, [k5, sl these 5 sts back to LH needle] twice, k3tog, ssk, psso.

BAG

With smaller needles, beg at top edge, cast on 76 sts. Work in k1, p1 rib for 4"/10cm, end with a RS row. Change to larger needles and p 1 row.

Beg chart pat

Row 1 (RS) Beg as indicated, work 12-st rep 6 times, end as indicated. Cont to foll chart in this way, rep rows 1-44 three times, rows 1-25 once. Change to smaller needles and p next row. Work in k1, p1 rib for 1"/2.5cm.

Eyelet row (RS) Work 29 sts, k2tog, yo, ssk, work 10 sts, k2tog, yo, ssk, work to end.

Next row *Work rib to eyelet, p1 and k1 in next yo; rep from * once, rib to end. Work even until rib measures 4"/10cm. Bind off in rib.

I-CORD

With dpn, cast on 2 sts.

***Next row (RS)** K2, do not turn. Slide sts to beg of needle to work next row from RS; rep from * until I-cord measures 50"/127cm. Bind off.

FINISHING

Block to measurements. Fold bag in half and sew side seams leaving 2 sts free for side gussets. Fold over rib trim at top and sew in place. Pull I-cord through eyelet opening and knot once at back. Pull one end through side gusset at left bottom edge and knot, then at right bottom edge and knot.

Stitch key

■ K on RS, p on WS

▬ P on RS, k on WS

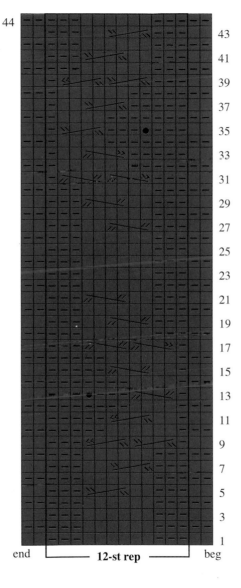 4-st RC

 4-st RPC

 4-st LC

 4-st LPC

● MB

end └─── **12-st rep** ───┘ beg

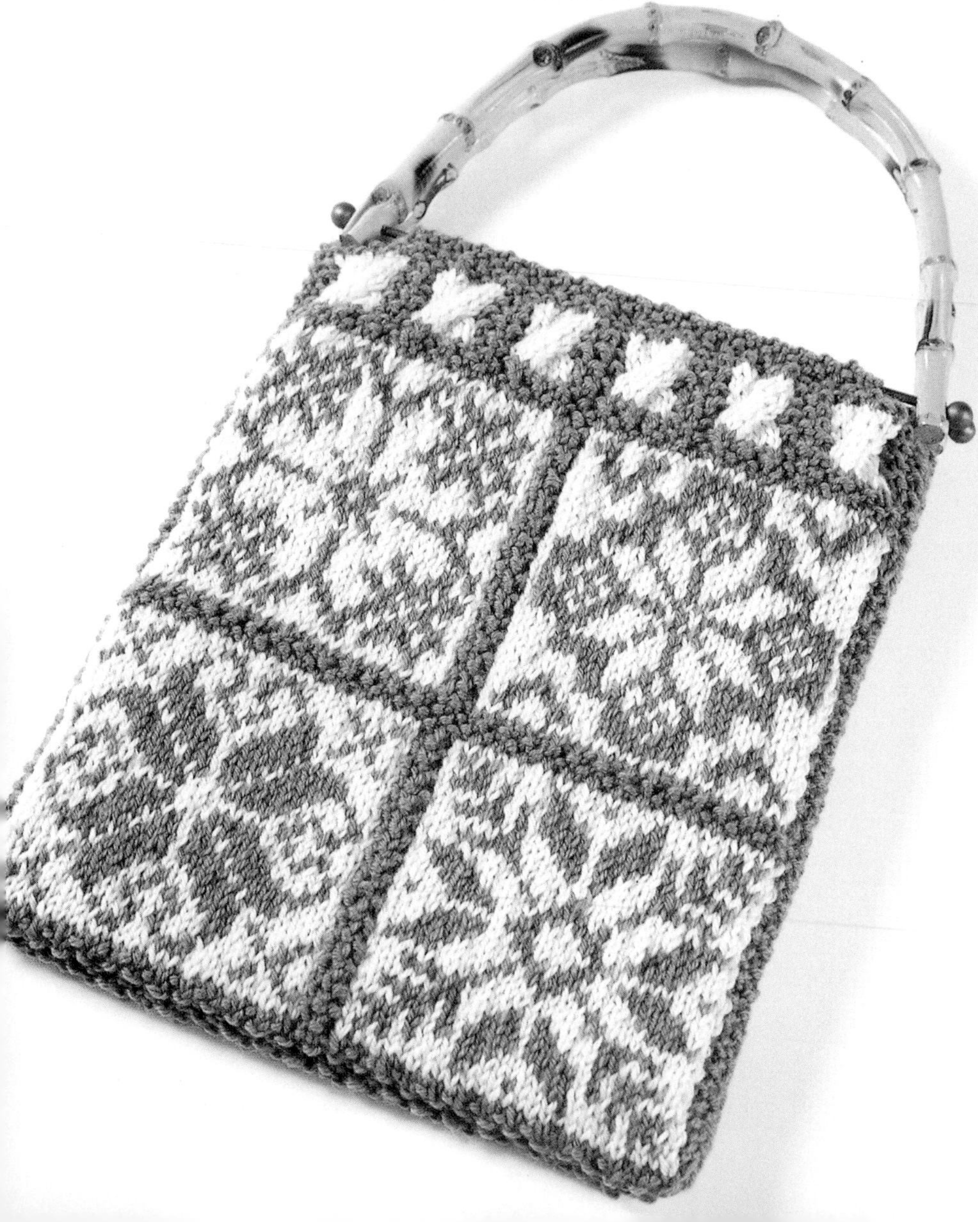

Bright white snowflakes accented with seed stitch and framed with mini-cables add up to a fun-to-knit bag. Contrasting bamboo handles provide the perfect finishing. Designed by Rebecca Rosen.

KNITTED MEASUREMENTS

- Approx 11½" x 10"/29cm x 25.5cm

MATERIALS

- 2 1¾oz/50g balls (each approx 131yd/118m) of K1C2, LLC *Cream Brulee DK* (wool ④) in #615 blue (MC)
- 1 ball in #101 ecru (CC)
- One pair size 6 (4mm) needles *or size to obtain gauge*
- Cable needle
- 1 set bamboo handles by Judi and Co.

GAUGES

- One snowflake square of 27 sts by 27 rows in St st using size 6 (4mm) needles measures 4½"/11.5cm wide by 4¼"/11cm long.
- 20 sts and 34 rows to 4"/10cm over seed st using size 6 (4mm) needles.

Take time to check gauges.

STITCH GLOSSARY

SEED STITCH
(over an odd number of sts)
Row 1 K1, *p1, k1; rep from * to end.
Row 2 K the purl and p the knit sts.
Rep row 2 for seed st.

CABLE PATTERN
(over 6 sts)
Rows 1, 3 and 7 (RS) Knit. **Rows 2, 4, 6 and 8** Purl. **Row 5** Sl 3 sts to cn and hold to *back*, k3, k3 from cn.

FRONT

With MC, cast on 65 sts.
Row 1 (RS) K1 (selvage st), work seed st to last st, k1 (selvage st). Cont to work selvage sts every row, work even in seed st for 3 more rows.

Beg chart pats
Row 1 (RS) K1 (selvage st), work 3 sts with MC in seed st, k27 with CC foll chart 1, work 3 sts with MC in seed st, k27 with CC foll chart 2, work 3 sts with MC in seed st, k1 (selvage st). Cont to work in this way until row 27 of charts is completed.
Row 28 (WS) With MC, k1, [work 3 sts in seed st, p27] twice work 3 sts in seed st, k1. Work 3 more rows with MC in seed st. Rep row 28.

Beg chart pats
Row 1 (RS) With MC k1, work 3 sts in seed st, k27 with CC foll chart 3, work 3 sts with MC in seed st, k27 with CC foll chart 4, work 3 sts with MC in seed st, k1. Cont in this way until row 27 of charts is completed. **Next row (WS)** With MC, k1 [work 3 sts in seed st, p11, p2tog, p12, p2tog] twice, work 3 sts in seed st, k1—61 sts. Work 4 more rows with MC in seed st, dec 2 sts on last WS row—59 sts. **Next row (RS)** K1, *work 3 sts with MC in seed st, k6 with CC (for row 1 of cable pat); rep from * 5 times more, work 3 sts with MC in seed st, k1. Cont to work in this way until 8 rows of cable pat are completed. **Next row (RS)** With MC, k1, M1 st, *work 3 sts in seed st, k6; rep from * 5 times more, work 3 sts with MC in seed st, M1 st, k1—61sts. Work 3 more rows in seed st. Bind off sts.

BACK

With MC, cast on 52 sts.

Row 1 (RS) K1 (selvage st), work 50 sts in seed st, k1 (selvage st). Cont to work in this way until piece measures same as front. Bind off sts tightly.

FINISHING

Block pieces to measurements. Sew lower and side seams firmly. Place markers at 1½"/4cm from each side seam on front for casing. Pick up and k 36 sts between markers. Work in seed st for 4 rows. Bind off. Fold casing over one handle and sew tightly in place. Work back casing in same way.

CHART 1

CHART 2

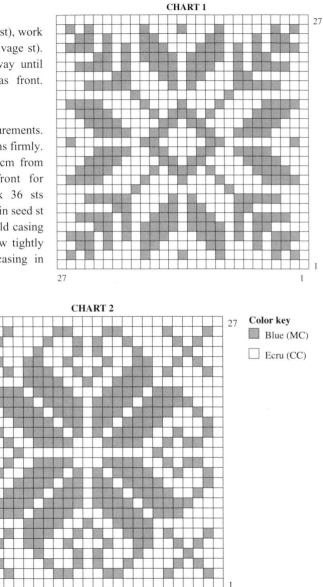

Color key

☐ Blue (MC)

☐ Ecru (CC)

CHART 3

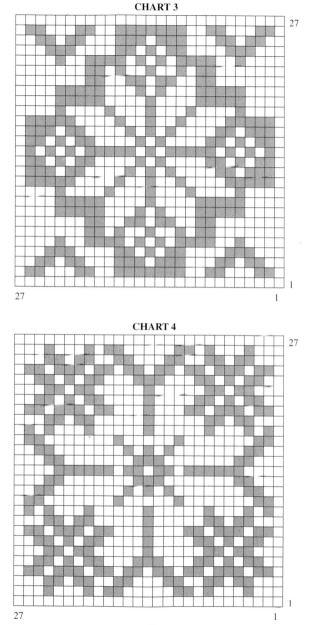

CHART 4

TIGER STRIPE PURSE

Animal instinct

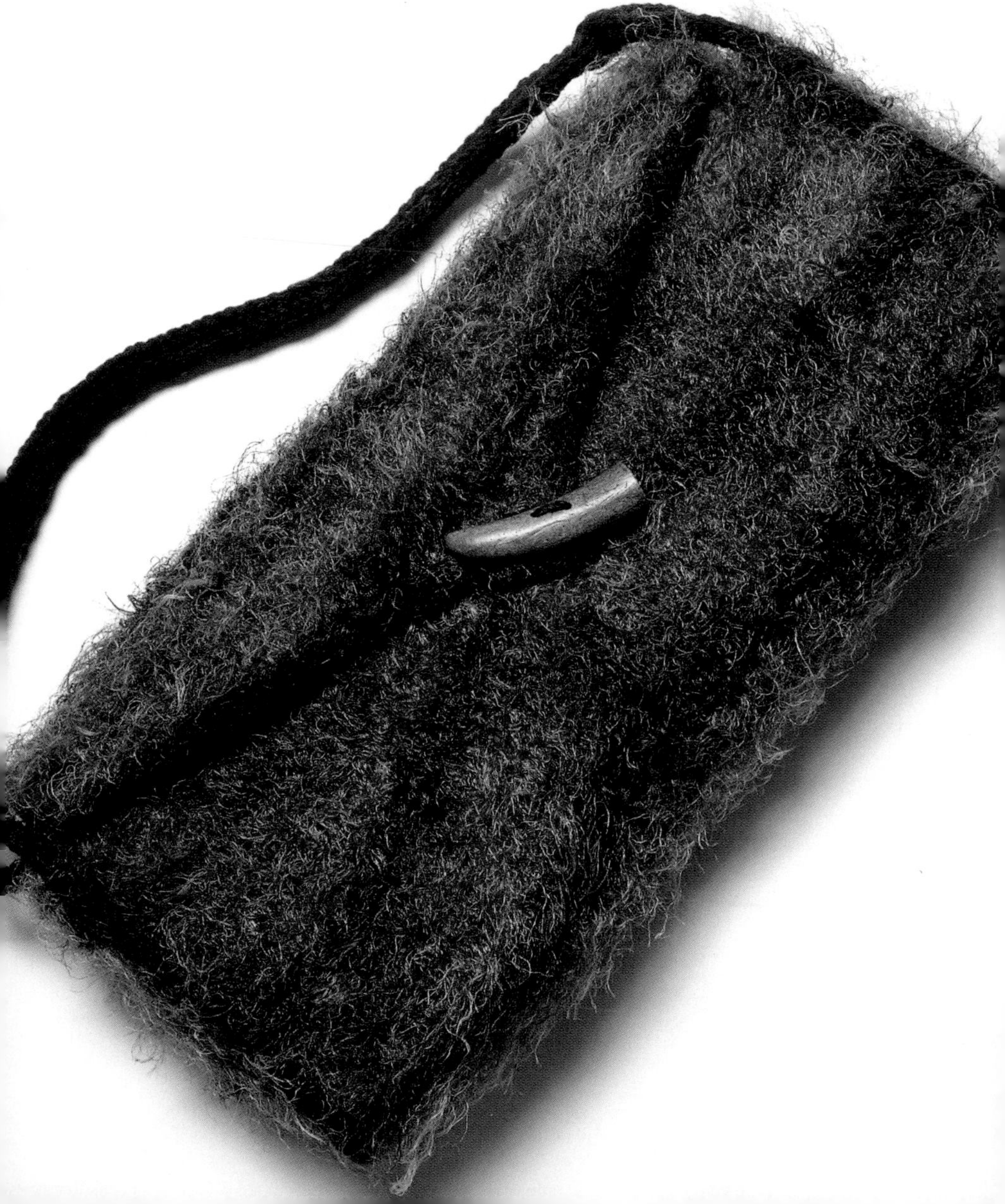

Plush hand-painted yarn creates a faux-fur surface for a baguette style handbag. It's finished with a cord handle, chain-loop gusset and horn toggle closure. Designed by Barbara Venishnick.

KNITTED MEASUREMENTS

▓ Approx 7" x 14"/18cm x 35.5cm

MATERIALS

▓ 1 4oz/125g hank (each approx 230yd/212m) of Cherry Tree Hill *Faux Fur* (nylon techno hair ④) each in java (A) and black (B)

▓ 1 4oz/125g hank (each approx 280yd/258m) of *Merino* (wool ④) in black (C)

▓ One pair size 4 (3.5mm) needles *or size to obtain gauge*

▓ Size 4 (3.5mm) circular needle, 29"/74cm long

▓ Two size 4 (3.5mm) dpn

▓ ½yd/.5m nonwoven stiff interfacing

▓ ½yd/.5m felted lining material

▓ One 2"/50mm toggle button

GAUGE

18 sts and 30 rows to 4"/10cm over St st foll charts using size 4 (3.5mm) needles. *Take time to check gauge.*

NOTE

Purse is knit in two long strips that are sewn tog at the center. Tiger stripe pat is achieved not by carrying colors but by working short rows so that only one color is worked at a time. (See chart and instructions).

STRIP I

With A, cast on 30 sts.

Beg chart I

Row I (RS) With A, knit (foll chart from right to left).

Row 2 With A, purl (foll chart from left to right.)

Row 3 With A, k23, turn.

Row 4 With A, p23.

Row 5 With A, k16, turn.

Row 6 With A, purl.

Row 7 With A, k9, turn.

Row 8 With A, purl.

Row 9 With B, k30.

Row 10 With B, p30.

Row II With A, k30.

Next row With A, p7, turn.

Next row With A, knit.

Cont to foll chart 1 in this way working short rows first at beg then at end of rows, until all 36 rows of chart are completed. Then rep rows 1-36 twice more, work rows 1-12 once. Cont to foll chart, bind off 4 sts at beg of every RS (knit) row 6 times. Bind off rem 6 sts.

STRIP 2

With A, cast on 30 sts. Work as for strip 1 ONLY in reverse, that is read RS rows from left to right and WS rows from right to left as foll:

Row I (WS) With A, purl.

Row 2 With A, knit. Work as for strip 1 reversing chart reading in this way and reversing shaping at flap by binding off 4 sts at beg of every WS (purl) row 6 times. Bind off rem 6 sts.

SIDE GUSSETS (make 2)

With A, cast on 16 sts. Foll chart 2 for short rows, working odd RS rows from right to left and even WS rows from left to right, work rows 1-22 twice, then rows 1-4 once. Bind off.

FINISHING

Block pieces to measurements. Foll assembly diagram, lay strips 1 and 2 beside each other with RS up and sew center seams tog. Foll diagram, pin or baste gusset to front bottom and back edges leaving the 2"/5cm of flap free. Rep for gusset on opposite side. With circular needle and C from RS, going through both layers of basted pieces, beg at top left edge on front, pick up and k 30 sts along front edge, 15 sts along bottom edge, 30 sts along back edge, then working through single layer on flap, 15 sts along straight edge of flap, 30 sts along slanted edge, cast on 9 sts for buttonloop, pick up 30 sts along other slanted edge, 15 sts along straight edge of flap, 30 sts through both layers on back of purse, 15 sts along bottom edge and 30 sts along front edge – 249 sts. Turn and k 1 row on all sts. P 1 row, k 1 row, p 1 row, k 1 row. Bind off.

I-CORD HANDLE

With dpn and C, cast on 4 sts.

*Next row (RS)** K4, do not turn. Slide sts to beg of needle to work next row from RS; rep from * until I-cord measures 25"/63.5cm. Bind off. Make a second I-cord in same way. Holding two I-cords tog, tie a square knot at one end at 2½"/6cm from one end leaving the 2 ends

free. Rep on opposite end. Sew the 2 ends to the front and back rolled trim, tucking under and securing tightly. Sew tog the two I-cords between square knots to make a doubled handle (see photo). Sew on button to front.

Interfacing and Lining

Cut one piece of interfacing 12"/30.5cm long x 3¼"/8cm wide for bottom. Cut 2 pieces 12"/30.5cm wide x 5½"/14cm tall for back and front. Sew back and front pieces to bottom and tack whole piece to inside of purse. For lining, cut bottom and front as for interfacing. For back and flap, cut one piece 12"/30.5cm wide and 10"/25.5cm long to reach the flap point. Sew pieces tog as for interfacing. Trim the corners to fit the flap point and turn under ¼"/.5cm. Place lining on bag with wrong sides together and slip stitch lining to inside of flap and to top edge of point.

Assembly Diagram

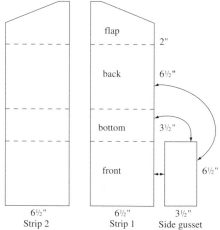

CHART 1

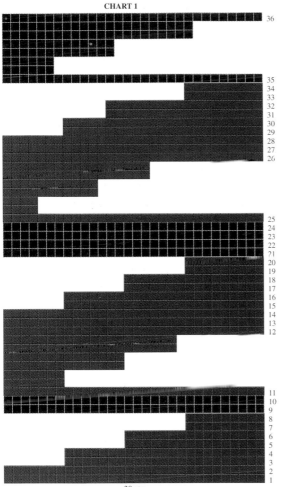

36

35
34
33
32
31
30
29
28
27
26

25
24
23
22
21
20
19
18
17
16
15
14
13
12

11
10
9
8
7
6
5
4
3
2
1

30 sts

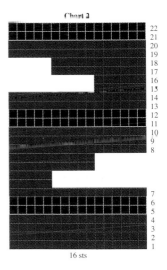

Chart 2

22
21
20
19
18
17
16
15
14
13
12
11
10
9
8

7
6
5
4
3
2
1

16 sts

Fisherman's friend

Trellis cables amid traditional diamond patterns, textural seed stitch and nail-head bobbles combine to form this handsome Aran pouch. Double pull cords close the mesh top. Designed by Jane Livingston.

KNITTED MEASUREMENTS

■ Approx 11" x 9½"/22cm x 24cm

MATERIALS

■ 4 1¾oz/50g balls (each approx 55yd/50m) of Berroco, Inc. *Pronto* (cotton/acrylic ⑤) in #4401 ecru

■ One pair each sizes 10 and 11 (6 and 8mm) needles *or size to obtain gauge*

■ Cable needle

GAUGE

14 sts and 21 rows to 4"/10cm over St st using smaller needles.
Take time to check gauge.

STITCH GLOSSARY

RT—Sk next st on LH needle, K next st in front of first st, then k first st and drop both sts from LH needle.

3-st RC—Sl 1 st to cn and hold to *back*, k2, k1 from cn.

3-st LC—Sl 2 sts to cn and hold to *front*, k1, k2 from cn.

3-st RPT—Sl 1 st to cn and hold to *back*, k2, p1 from cn.

3-st LPT—Sl 2 sts to cn and hold to *front*, p1, k2 from cn.

4-st RC (LC)—Sl 2 sts to cn and hold to *back (front)*, k2, k2 from cn.

4-st RPT—Sl 2 sts to cn and hold to *back*, k2, p2 from cn.

4-st LPT—Sl 2 sts to cn and hold to *front*, p2, k2 from cn.

K2/K1/P1RT—Sl 2 sts to cn and hold to *back*, k2; k1, p1 from cn.

P1/K1/K2LT—Sl 2 sts to cn and hold to *front*, p1, k1; k2 from cn.

5-st RPT—Sl 3 sts to cn and hold to *back*, k2; work p1, k2 from cn.

Dec Cable —Sl 2 sts to cn and hold to *back*, k2tog; k2tog from cn.

MB—Make bobble as foll: insert RH needle into next 2 sts as if to k2tog and work (k1, yo, k1, yo and k1) in these 2 sts to make 5 sts, turn, p5, turn, ssk, k1, k2tog, turn, p3, turn—2 sts rem.

BAG

With larger needles, cast on 72 sts for top.
Rows 1 and 2 Knit. **Row 3 (RS)** K1, *yo, k2tog; rep from *, end k1. **Row 4** P2, *yo, p2tog; rep from * to end. Rep rows 3 and 4 twice more. Change to smaller needles.
Row 9 K2, *p2, k4; rep from *, end p2, k2. **Eyelet (inc) row 10** P2, *yo, k2tog, yo, p4; rep from *, end yo, k2tog, yo, p2—84 sts. **Row 11** K2, *p3, 4-st RC; rep from *, end p3, k2. **Rows 12-14** K the knit sts and p the purl sts. **Row 15** Rep row 11. **Row 16** P4, *k1, p4, k1, p8; rep from *, end [k1, p4] twice. **Row 17** P1, k1, p1, M1, p1, *p1, k4, p2, [k1, p1] twice, M1, p1, k1, p1; rep from *, end p1, k4, p2, M1, p1, k1, p1—91 sts. **Row 18** [P1, k1] twice, p1, *k1, p4, [k1, p1] 5 times; rep from *, end k1, p4, [k1, p1] 3 times. **Row 19** [P1, k1] twice, p1, *p1, 4-st RC, p2, [k1, p1] 4 times; rep from *, end p1, 4-st RC, p2, [k1, p1] twice. **Row 20** Rep row 18. **Row 21** [P1,

k1] twice, p1, *p1, k4, p2, [k1, p1] 4 times; rep from *, end p1, k4, p2, [k1, p1] twice. **Rows 22 and 24** Rep row 18. **Row 23** Rep row 19. **Row 25** [P1, k1] twice, 4-st RPT, 4-st LPT, k1, [p1, k1] 3 times; rep from *, end 4-st RPT, 4-st LPT, [k1, p1] twice. **Row 26** [P1, k1] twice, *p2, k4, p2, k1, [p1, k1] 3 times; rep from *, end p2, k4, p2, [k1, p1] twice. **Row 27** P1, k1, *4-st RPT, p4, 4-st LPT, k1 p1, k1; rep from *, end 4-st RPT, p4, 4-st LPT, k1, p1. **Row 28** P1, k1, *p2, k8, p2, k1, p1, k1; rep from *, end p2, k8, p2, k1, p1. **Row 29** *P1, 3-st RPT, p3, MB over next 2 sts, p3, 3-st LPT; rep from *, end p1. **Row 30** *P3, k4, p2, k4, p2; rep from *, end p1. **Row 31** P1, k2, *p4, RT, p4, 5-st RPT; rep from *, end p4, RT, p4, k2, p1. **Rows 32, 34, 36 and 38** P1, *p2, k4, p2, k4, p2, k1; rep from *, end p1. **Rows 33 and 35** P1, *k2, p4, RT, p4, k2, p1; rep from * to end. **Row 37** Rep row 31. **Row 39** P1, *3-st LC, p3, MB, p3, 3-st RC, p1; rep from * to end. **Row 40** P1, k1, *p2, k8, p2, k1, p1, k1; rep from *, end p2, k8, p2, k1, p1. **Row 41** P1, k1, *P1/K1/K2LT, p4, K2/K1/P1RT, k1, p1, k1; rep from *, end k1, p1. **Row 42** [P1, k1] twice, *p2, k4, p2, k1, [p1, k1] 3 times; rep from *, end p2, k4, p2, [k1, p1] twice. **Row 43** *[P1, k1] twice, 4-st LPT, 4-st RPT, k1, p1, k1; rep from *, end p1. **Row 44** *[P1, k1] 3 times, p4, [k1, p1] twice, k1; rep from *, end p1. **Rows 45 and 49** Rep row 19. **Rows 46, 48, 50 and 52** Rep row 18. **Rows 47 and 51** Rep row

21. **Row 53** *P1, k1, p1, k2tog, p1, 4-st BC, p1, ssk, p1, k1; rep from *, end p1— 79 sts. **Row 54** P1, k1, p1, *p1, k1, p4, k1, p2, [k1, p1] twice; rep from *, end p1, k1, p4, k1, p2, k1, p1. **Row 55** P1, *[k1, p1] twice, k4, [p1, k1] twice, p1; rep from * to end. **Row 56** P1, *k1, p2, k1, p4, k1, p2, k1, p1; rep from * to end. **Row 57** P1, *k1, k2tog, p1, 4-st BC, p1, ssk, k1, p1; rep from * to end—67 sts. **Row 58** P1, *k1, p1, k1, p4, [k1, p1] twice; rep from * to end. **Row 59** P1, *k2tog, p1, k4, p1, ssk, p1; rep from * to end—55 sts. **Row 60** P1, *p1, k1, p4, k1, p2; rep from * to end. **Row 61** K2tog, p1, *dec cable, p1, SK2P, p1; rep from *, end dec cable, p1, ssk—31 sts. **Row 62** P2tog, *p3tog, p2tog; rep from *, end p3tog, p1—13 sts.

Cut yarn. Draw 2 strands of yarn through rem sts and pull tog tightly. Sew side seam from the top down, reversing the seam of the first 3"/7.5cm (lace section) for turn-back.

I-cord drawstring
(make 2)
With 2 dpn and single strand MC, cast on 3 sts. ***Next row** K3, do not turn. Slide sts to beg of needle to work the next row from the RS; rep from * until I-cord measures 30"/76cm. Bind off.

FINISHING
Sew one I-cord through alternate eyelet holes of eyelet row in one direction and the other I-cord in the opposite direction. Knot ends tog.

ROSEBUD LACE TRAVEL BAG
Budding beauty

Extravagant styling and embellishment are the hallmark of this spectacular drawstring lingerie bag. Beginning with a spiral circular base, the bag's worked in trellis and vine patterns, then trimmed with a picot edge and delicate beads. Designed by Sasha Kagan.

KNITTED MEASUREMENTS

■ Approx 10" x 8"/25.5cm x 20.5cm

MATERIALS

■ 2 1¾oz/50g balls (each approx 187yd/170m) of Rowan/Westminster Fibers *4 Ply Cotton* (cotton ②) in #114 violet (MC)

■ 1 ball each in #106 magenta (A) and #120 orchid (E)

■ 1 1¾oz/50g ball (each approx 127yd/115m) of *Cotton Glacé* (cotton ③) each in #797 lagoon (B) and #724 bubbles (C)

■ 1 1¾oz/50g ball (each approx 176yd/1160m) of *Fine Cotton Chenille* (cotton ③) each in #408 crocus (D) and #414 ecru (F)

■ One pair each sizes 2 and 4 (2.5 and 3.5mm) needles *or size to obtain gauge*

■ One set (5) size 4 (3.5mm) dpn

■ Size 5 steel (1.75mm) crochet hook

■ 1 pkg dk blue bugle beads

■ 1 pkg mother-of-pearl small round beads

■ 7¾"/19.5cm diameter cardboard circle

■ ½yd/.5m silk for lining

GAUGE

24 sts and 32 rows to 4"/10 cm over body pat st using larger needles.
Take time to check gauge.

LITTLE VINE PATTERN

(over 10 sts)
Row 1 (RS) K4, yo, k1, ssk, k3. **Row 2** P2, p2tog tbl, p1, yo, p5. **Row 3** K6, yo, k1, ssk, k1. **Row 4** P2tog tbl, p1, yo, p7. **Row 5** K3, k2tog, k1, yo, k4. **Row 6** P5, yo, p1, p2tog, p2. **Row 7** K1, k2tog, k1, yo, k6. **Row 8** P7, yo, p1, p2tog. Rep rows 1-8 for little vine pat.

BASE

With dpn and MC, cast on 8 sts. Join and divide sts onto 4 dpn.
Rnd 1 [Yo, k1] 8 times. **Rnd 2** [Yo, k2tog] 8 times. **Rnd 3** [Yo, k2] 8 times. **Rnd 4** [Yo, k1, k2tog] 8 times. **Rnd 5** [Yo, k3] 8 times. **Rnd 6** [Yo, k2, k2tog] 8 times. **Rnd 7** [Yo, k4] 8 times. **Rnd 8** [Yo, k3, k2tog] 8 times. **Rnd 9** [Yo, k5] 8 times. **Rnd 10** [Yo, k4, k2tog] 8 times. **Rnd 11** [Yo, k6] 8 times. **Rnd 12** [Yo, k5, k2tog] 8 times. **Rnd 13** [Yo, k7] 8 times. **Rnd 14** [Yo, k6, k2tog] 8 times. **Rnd 15** [Yo, k8] 8 times. **Rnd 16** [Yo, k7, k2tog] 8 times. **Rnd 17** [Yo, k9] 8 times. **Rnd 18** [Yo, k8, k2tog] 8 times. **Rnd 19** [Yo, k10] 8 times. **Rnd 20** [Yo, k9, k2tog] 8 times. **Rnd 21** [Yo, k11] 8 times. **Rnd 22** [Yo, k10, k2tog] 8 times. **Rnd 23** [Yo, k12] 8 times. **Rnd 24** [Yo, k11, k2tog] 8 times. **Rnd 25** [Yo, k13] 8 times. **Rnd 26** [Yo, k12, k2tog] 8 times. **Rnd 27** [Yo, k14] 8 times. **Rnd 28** [Yo, k13, k2tog] 8 times. **Rnd 29** [Yo, k15] 8 times. **Rnd 30** [Yo, k14, k2tog] 8 times. **Rnd 31** [Yo, k16] 8 times. **Rnd 32** [Yo, k15, k2tog] 8 times. **Rnd 33** [Yo, k17] 8 times. **Rnd 34** [Yo, k16, k2tog] 8 times. **Rnd 35** [Yo, k18] 8 times. **Rnd 36** [Yo, k16, k2tog] 8 times.
Circumference of circle measures approx 26"/66cm. Bind off.

BAG SIDES

With smaller needles and A, cast on 150 sts. K 2 rows A, 2 rows B, 2 rows C, 2 rows D and 2 rows A. Change to larger needles.

Beg chart pat

Row 1 (RS) Work 50-st rep 3 times. Cont to foll chart through row 32. Then rep rows 1-32 once more. With MC, k 1 row, p 1 row. **Next (eyelet) row** *K4, yo, k2tog; rep from * to end. [P 1 row, k 1 row] twice. **Next row (WS of pat)** Beg with row 1, work little vine pat over all 150 sts. (Thus, WS and RS of pat are reversed for bag drawstring top). Cont in this way until 16 rows of pat have been worked. Change to smaller needles. K 2 rows D, 2 rows A. Bind off.

FINISHING

Block pieces to measurements. Sew side seam of bag. Sew bag sides to base.

Picot edge

Beg at top edge seam, with crochet hook and A, join and ch 3, sl st in same st with joining, *work sl st in next 3 sts, ch 3, sl st in last sl st worked; rep from * around. Work picot edge in same way into the A rnd at bottom of bag and base joining.

Beading

Along picot edge, with matching sewing thread, sew 3 pearl beads in each picot and one bugle bead into 3 sl st space.

Lining

Cover cardboard circle with lining. Cut a 10" x 27"/25.5cm x 68.5cm length of fabric for lining. Sew lining to base. Tack top of lining to bag just below eyelet row. Make a 42"/107cm twisted cord with colors A, B, C, D and E. Knot ends and cover knot with a circle of bugle beads trimmed at top and bottom with pearls.

Color key

- ▨ Violet (MC)
- ■ Magenta (A)
- ▨ Lagoon (B)
- ▧ Bubbles (C)
- ■ Crocus (D)
- ▨ Orchid (E)
- ☐ Ecru (F)

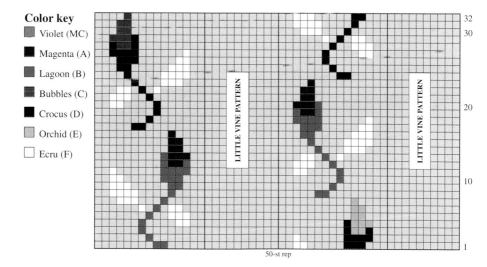

LITTLE VINE PATTERN

LITTLE VINE PATTERN

50-st rep

STRIPED MONEY POUCH

Small change

Shiny rayon yarn adds evening glamour. The scaled-down backpack closing makes a modern statement on this side-ways striped mini evening bag. Designed by Karin Skacel Haack.

KNITTED MEASUREMENTS

■ Approx 7" x 5"/18cm x 12.5cm

MATERIALS

■ 1 1¾oz/50g cone (each approx 85yd/76.5m) of Skacel Collection *Hillary* (rayon ④) each in #1 white (MC) and #2 black (CC)

■ One pair size 6 (4mm) needles *or size to obtain gauge.*

■ One set (5) size 6 (4mm) dpn

GAUGE

20 sts and 32 rows to 4"/10 cm over St st using size 6 (4mm) needles

Take time to check gauge.

Note Stripe pat is formed by working short rows.

POUCH SIDES

With MC, cast on 40 sts. Work in St st for 2 rows.

*Next row (RS) With CC, k16, sl next st from LH needle to RH needle, bring yarn to front, then sl st back to LH needle. Turn work and p16 with CC. With MC, work 4 rows in St st over all sts.

Next row With CC, k32, turn work (do *not* sl yarn to prevent holes. The holes will be for drawstring to pull through).

Next row With CC, p32. With MC, work 4 rows in St st over all sts.* Rep between

*'s 8 times more, only work 2 rows with MC instead of 4 rows at end of last rep. Bind off. Sew cast-on and bound-off edges tog to form back seam.

CIRCLE BASE

With CC and dpn, pick up and k 60 sts around lower edge of pouch, dividing sts evenly on 4 needles (15 sts on each needle).
Rnd 1 Knit. **Rnd 2** Purl. **Rnd 3** *K2tog, k to last 2 sts on needle, k2tog; rep from * around on each needle (8 sts dec'd)—52 sts.
Rnd 4 Knit. **Rnd 5** Rep rnd 3—44 sts.
Rnd 6 Knit. **Rnd 7** Rep rnd 3—36 sts.
Rnd 8 Knit. **Rnd 9** Rep rnd 3—28 sts.
Rnd 10 Knit. **Rnd 11** Rep rnd 3—20 sts.
Rnd 12 Knit. **Rnd 13** Rep rnd 3—12 sts.
Rnd 14 Knit.
Pull yarn through rem sts on needles and draw up tightly to secure.

FINISHING

Block bag lightly, top edge will roll naturally to inside edge.

I-cord

With dpn, cast on 4 sts.
*Next row (RS) K4, do not turn. Slide sts to beg of needle to work next row from RS; rep from * until I-cord measures 110"/280cm. Bind off.
To trim lower base and make drawstring, beg at back seam, sew I-cord trim around base, then thread in and out through top short row holes, then out same hole as beg, then sew end to base at same place as beg of I-cord. Pull drawstring to tighten top.

ROSE-ENCRUSTED BAG

Some enchanted evening

For Experienced Knitters

Intricate, individually-knit rose and leaf appliqués take a simple drawstring bag from simple to spectacular. The delicate I-cord features a unique knit-in twist. Designed by Nicky Epstein.

KNITTED MEASUREMENTS
- Approx 7" x 5"/18cm x 12.5cm

MATERIALS
- 2 1¾oz/50g balls (each approx 167yd/155m) of Lang *Opal* (rayon ①) each in #4226 sand (MC) and #4294 ecru (CC)
- One pair each sizes 2 and 4 (2.5 and 3.5mm) needles *or size to obtain gauge*
- Two size 2 (2.5mm) dpn
- Cable needle
- 8"/20.5cm of ½"/13mm wide ribbon

GAUGE
23 sts and 38 rows to 4"/10cm over St st using double strand and larger needles. *Take time to check gauge.*

ROSES (make 17)
With smaller needles and single strand CC, cast on 37 sts. **Row I (RS)** K1, *p1, k1; rep from * to end. **Rows 2, 4, 6, 8 and 10** K the knit and p the purl sts. **Row 3** K1, *p1, M1 purlwise, k1; rep from * to end. **Row 5** K1, *p2, M1 purlwise, k1; rep from * to end. Cont in this way to inc 18 sts every other row until there are 109 sts. Bind off. Roll ruffle edge from outside and sew along cast-on edge to form a rose.

LEAVES (make 17)
With smaller needles and single strand MC, cast on 15 sts. **Row I (RS)** K6, sl2tog knitwise, k1, p2sso, (S2K1P), k6. **Row 2** K6, p1, k6. **Row 3** K5, S2K1P, k5. **Row 4** K5,

p1, k5. **Row 5** K4, S2K1P, k4. **Row 6** K4, p1, k4. **Row 7** K3, S2K1P, k3. **Row 8** K3, p1, k3. **Row 9** K2, S2K1P, k2. **Row 10** K2, p1, k2. **Row 11** K1, S2K1P, k1. **Row 12** K1, p1, k1. **Row 13** S2K1P. Fasten off last st.

BAG BODY
With larger needles and double strand MC, cast on 69 sts. Work in St st until piece measures 5½"/14cm. Change to smaller needles and single strand of MC and work in k1, p1 rib for ¾"/2cm. Then, work rows 3-9 of roses. Bind off in pat.

BAG BOTTOM
With RS facing, larger needles and double strand MC, pick up and k 70 sts evenly around cast-on edge of body. P 1 row on WS. **Row I** *SK2P, k11, rep from * to end. **Row 2 and all WS rows** Purl. **Row 3** *SK2P, k9; rep from * to end.Cont in this way to dec 10 sts every other row until 10 sts rem. **Row 13** K2tog across—5 sts. Cut yarn and thread through sts on needle. Draw up tightly and secure.

Cabled I-cord drawstring
With 2 dpn and single strand MC, cast on 5 sts. *Row I K5. Do not turn. Slide sts to beg of needle to work next row from RS; rep from * 3 times more. **Row 5 (RS)** K1, sl 1 st to cn and hold to *front*, k2, k1 from cn, k1. Rep rows 1-5 for cabled I-cord until cord measures 34"/86cm. Bind off. Make a 2nd 8"/20.5cm cabled I-cord for strap.

FINISHING
Block bag to measurements. Foll photo, sew 15 roses and 14 leaves to bag. Sew lower and back seams. Use ribbon to form a drawstring casing at inside of ribbed edge. Pull drawstring through casing and sew rem roses and leaves to cord ends.

ROMANCE REVISITED

Purls and pearls

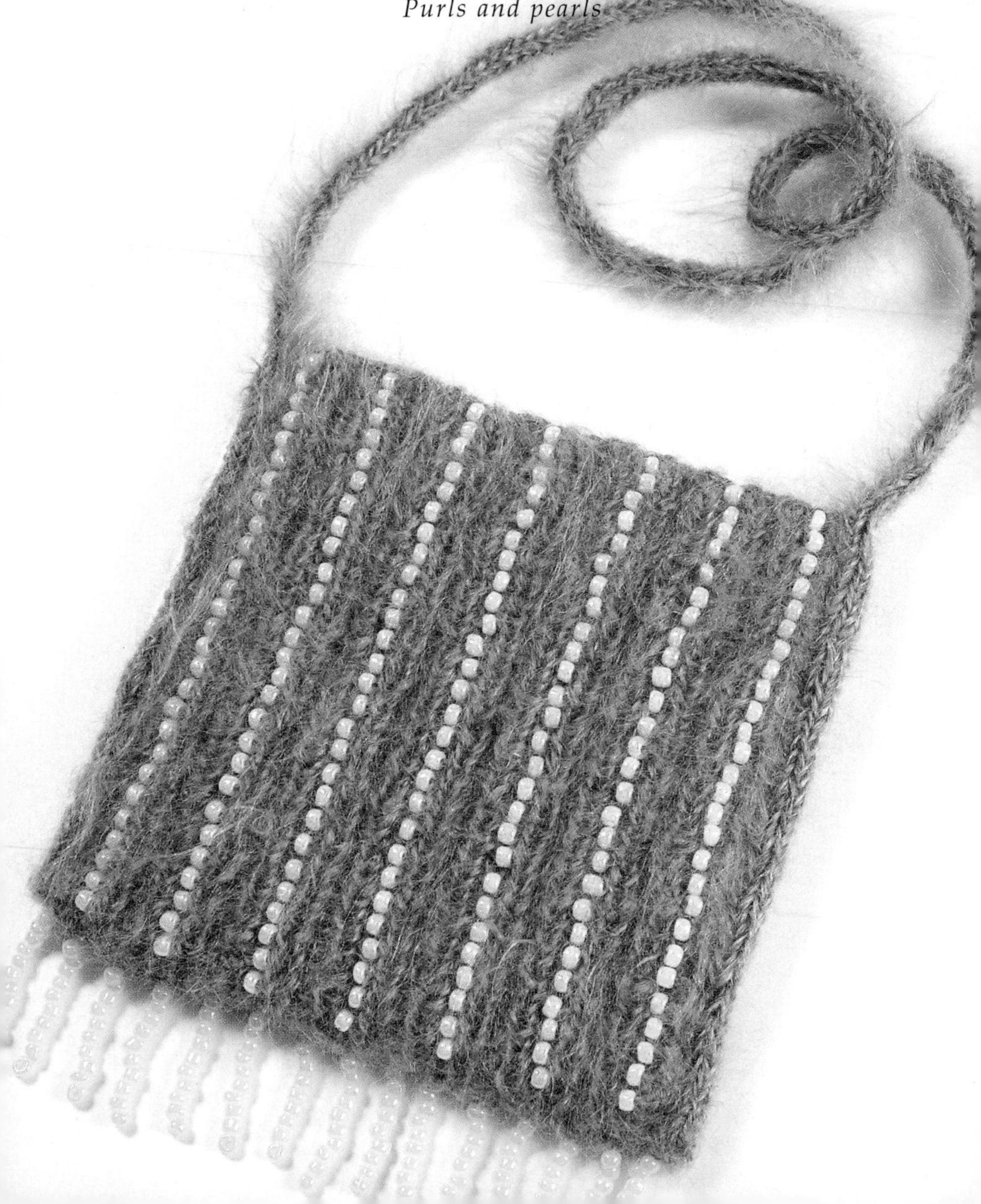

Luxurious mohair encrusted with rows of knit-in pearl beads and strung fringe creates an elegant evening bag—the shoulder strap is a simple I-cord. Designed by Rosemary Drysdale.

KNITTED MEASUREMENTS
- Approx 7" x 7½"/18cm x 19cm

MATERIALS
- 1 1¾oz/50g balls (each approx 98yd/90m) of Filatura Di Crosa *Mohair Lungo* (mohair/wool ⑤) in #602 blue
- Glass beads
- One pair size 5 (3.75mm) needles *or size to obtain gauge*
- Two size 4 (3.5mm) dpn (for I-cord)

GAUGE
20 sts and 26 rows to 4"/10 cm over k3, p2 rib using size 5 (3.75mm) needles.
Take time to check gauge.

Note K1 at beg and end of every row for selvage st.

STITCH GLOSSARY
K3, P2 RIB
Row 1 *K3, p2; rep from * to end.
Row 2 K the knit sts and p the purl sts.
Rep row 2 for k3, p2 rib.

ATTACH BEAD
Wyif, slip bead up to st, sl 1 purlwise, bring yarn to back.

FRONT
String 189 beads onto yarn before beg to knit.
Cast on 35 sts.
Row 1 K1 (selvage st), *k3, p2; rep from *, end k3, k1 (selvage st). Work 1 row even.
Row 3 K1 (selvage st), *k1, attach bead, k1, p2; rep from *, end k1, k1 (selvage st). Work 1 row even.
Rep last 2 rows until piece measures 7½"/19cm. Bind off loosely.

BACK
Work as for front omitting beads.

I-CORD
With dpn, cast on 4 sts.
***Next row (RS)** K4, do not turn. Slide sts to beg of needle to work next row from RS; rep from * until I-cord measures 46"/116.5cm. Bind off.

FINISHING
Sew front and back tog on 3 sides, leaving top open. Attach I-cord to sides.
Beaded fringe
Make 15 strings of 10 beads each and attach to bottom of bag.

A study in textures, this mini-bag, knit in rayon cord and embroidered with ombré rayon curly ribbon, is finished with a matching lining and twisted cable handle. Designed by Judi Alweil.

KNITTED MEASUREMENTS

■ Approx 7" x 8"/18cm x 20.5cm

MATERIALS

■ 1 1¾oz/50g spool (each approx 144yd/130m) of Judi & Co.'s *Cordé* (rayon ④) in olive (MC)
■ 6½yd/5.95m of *Luminesse Hand Dyed Rayon Ribbon* (rayon ④) in brown iris (CC)
■ One pair size 5 (3.75mm) needles *or size to obtain gauge*
■ Cable needle
■ Magnetic snap
■ ½yd/.5m stiff lining material
■ Tapestry needle

GAUGE

18 sts and 28 rows to 4"/10cm over St st using size 5 (3.75mm) needles.
Take time to check gauge.

BACK

With MC, cast on 32 sts. Work in garter st for 12 rows. Work in St st for 10 rows. K next row on RS, inc 1 st each side—34 sts.

P 1 row. Work in garter st for 8 rows. K next row, inc 1 st each side—36 sts. K 1 row. Work in St st for 8 rows. K next row, inc 1 st each side—38 sts. P 1 row. Work in garter st for 6 rows.

STRAP

Bind off 14 sts, k until there are 10 sts from bind off, join 2nd ball or a short length of yarn and bind off rem 14 sts. Cont in garter st on 10 sts for strap for 1½"/4cm more.

Next row (RS) K5, join 2nd ball of yarn and k rem 5 sts. Work both sides separately for 2"/5cm.

Next row (RS) Sl first 5 sts to a cn and hold to front, k last 5 sts, k first 5 sts (for cable twist). Cont on all 10 sts for 1¼"/3cm more. Bind off.

FRONT

Work as for back.

FINISHING

Block pieces lightly. Using CC, embroider 3 lazy daisy flowers in upper St st section. Embroider 2 more flowers in lower section. Work other piece in same way. Cut 2 separate lining pieces with seam allowances using knit pieces as a guide. Finish 4 edges of lining and sew to inside of each piece. Whip stitch lower and side edges tog from RS. Whip st strap tog from WS.

Deborah Newton's brightly-hued dimensional chains add colorful contrast to a basic black backpack. Button fastening, gradated side gussets and a drawstring top provide dynamic design details.

KNITTED MEASUREMENTS
- Approx 12"/30.5cm square

MATERIALS
- 2 1¾oz/50g skeins (each approx 138yd/123m) of Classic Elite *Waterspun Felted 100% Merino Wool* (wool ③) in #5013 black (MC)
- 1 skein each in #5051 gold (A), #5005 pink (B), #5072 teal (C) and #5085 orange (D)
- One pair size 7 (4.5mm) needles *or size to obtain gauge*
- One each sizes 5 and 7 (3.75 and 4.5mm) circular needle, 16"/42cm long
- Two size 7 (4.5mm) dpn
- Three 1"/25mm buttons

GAUGE
21 sts and 36 rows to 4"/10cm over chain link pat st using size 7 (4.5mm) needles. *Take time to check gauge.*

CHAIN LINK PATTERN
(multiple of 8 sts plus 6)
Row 1 (RS) With MC, knit.
Row 2 With MC, purl.
Rows 3 and 4 With A, knit.
Row 5 With MC, k6, *sl 2 wyib, k6; rep from * to end.
Row 6 With MC, p6, *sl 2 wyif, p6; rep from * to end.

Row 7 With A, rep row 5.
Row 8 With A, knit.
Rows 9 and 10 With MC, rep rows 1 and 2.
Rows 11 and 12 With B, knit.
Row 13 With MC, k2, *sl 2 wyib, k6; rep from *, end sl 2 wyib, k2.
Row 14 With MC, p2, *sl 2 wyif, p6; rep from *, end sl 2 wyif, p2.
Row 15 With B, rep row 13.
Row 16 With B, knit.
Rows 17-32 Rep rows 1-16, substituting C for A and D for B.
Rep rows 1-32 for chain link pat.

MAIN SECTION
With MC cast on 118 sts. Work in chain link pat until piece measures 10"/25.5cm, ending with third C stripe and 2 rows with MC. Bind off. Along cast-on and bound-off rows, mark center 3"/7.5cm and place yarn markers each side of center.

SIDE GUSSETS
Along one edge from RS, with MC, pick up and k 16 sts between markers. P 1 row. Beg with pat row 3, work in chain link pat for 3½"/9cm. Dec 1 st each side of next RS row—14 sts. Cont in pat until piece measures 7"/18cm. Dec 1 st each side of next RS row—12 sts. Work even until piece measures 9½"/24cm and piece fits along side edge of bag, end with a WS row in MC. Bind off.
Work other side gusset between markers on other edge in same way. Block pieces lightly. Sew gussets to main section with MC so that seam shows on RS.

Top ribbing

With RS facing, smaller circular needle and B, pick up and k 132 sts around top opening of bag. Join and mark beg of rnd. Work in k2, p2 rib for ½"/1.25cm.
Eyelet rnd *K2, yo, p2tog, k2, p2; rep from * around.
Work even until rib measures 1"/2.5cm. With MC, rib 1 rnd, then bind off in rib.

FLAP

With RS of back of bag facing and MC, pick up and k 46 sts evenly along back edge. P 1 row on WS. Beg with pat row 3, work in chain link pat for 5¼"/13.5cm. Bind off 2 sts at beg of next 20 rows. Bind off rem 6 sts.

Flap trim

With RS facing, smaller circular needle and B, pick up and k 110 sts around entire flap edge. Change to larger circular needle and k 1 row, p 1 row. Bind off knitwise on WS.

BACK STRAPS

With MC, cast on 100 sts. K 1 row. With C, k 2 rows. With MC, k 2 rows forming a 4-st buttonhole (bind off 4 sts, then cast on 4 sts over bound-off sts on foll row) at 4 sts from one end. With D, k 2 rows. With MC, k 1 row and bind off. Work a second back strap substituting B for C and A for D.

BACK LOOP

With MC, cast on 20 sts. K 1 row. With C, k 2 rows. With MC, k 1 row. Bind off. Sew back loop to center back. Sew straps either side of back loop, then sew buttonhole ends to lower side gussets. Sew on a button to back opposite each strap buttonhole.

I-cord drawstring

With 2 dpn and MC, cast on 3 sts.
*Next row K3, do not turn. Slide sts to beg of needle to work next row from RS; rep from * until I-cord measures 36"/91.5cm. Bind off. Pull drawstring through eyelets in rib. Make a 2"/5cm I-cord for button-loop on flap. Sew to flap. Sew on button to front opposite loop.

PAISLEY CARRY-ALL

Carpetbag

Richly embroidered paislies pattern this sturdy structured and lined tote. Generous sizing, garter straps and a whimsical striped base coordinate to make this the perfect knitting bag for toting along your latest project. Designed by Kristen Nicholas.

KNITTED MEASUREMENTS
▪ Approx 40" x 46"/101.5cm x 117cm

MATERIALS
▪ 6 1¾oz/50g hanks (each approx 95yd/87m) of Classic Elite Tapestry (wool/mohair ④) each in #2203 grey (A) and #2266 marigold (B)
▪ 2 hanks each in #2210 navy (C) and #2235 green (D)
▪ 1 hank each in #2285 couscous (E) and #2234 raspberry (F)
▪ Size 6 (4mm) circular needle, 32"/80cm long *or size to obtain gauge*
▪ Bobbins
▪ Stitch marker
▪ 1¾yd/1.6m of webbing for handles
▪ ⅝yd/.6m buckram
▪ ½yd/.5m lining fabric

GAUGE
21 sts and 23 rows to 4"/10 cm over Fair Isle pat using size 6 (4mm) needle.
Take time to check gauge.

Notes 1) When changing colors, twist yarns on WS to prevent holes in work. Carry color not in use loosley across WS. **2)** Paisley motifs are worked with A. Contrasting colors are worked in duplicate st and French knots in desired colors (see photo and chart for inspiration.)

BAG
With C, cast on 126 sts. Join, taking care not to twist sts. Mark end of rnd and sl marker every rnd. P 2 rnds. Change to B and k 1 rnd, inc 14 sts evenly around—140 sts.

Beg paisley chart
Rnd 1 Work 14-st rep 10 times. Cont in this way through rnd 33, then rep rnds 2-33 once more. Work 2 rnds St st with B. Change to F and k 1 rnd, p 2 rnds.

Beg oval chart
Rnd 1 Work 20-st rep 7 times. Cont in this way through rnd 13. With F, k 1 rnd, p 2 rnds. Bind off knitwise.

FINISHING
With D, E and F, duplicate st center of paisley motif in desired colors. Then embroider French knots in center of paisleys using B, C, E, and F.

HANDLES (make 2)
With F, cast on 10 sts. Working back and forth in rows, work in garter st for 30"/76cm. Bind off.

BASE
With A cast on 50 sts. Work in rev St st as foll: 4 rows each A, D, F, C, B and A. Bind off knitwise in A. Sew base around bottom of bag.

FINISHING
Using ¾"/20mm webbing for handles, stitch handle around webbing. Attach to bag at opposite sides.

Cut a piece of buckram to fit around inside of bag. Baste in place. Cut a smaller piece for the base of bag and baste in place. Cut a piece of lining fabric enough to go around inside of bag with a 1"/2.5cm seam down 1 side and across the bottom. Sew. Turn down top edge and sew to inside of bag.

Trace bottom of bag and cut a piece of cardboard to reinforce bottom. Cut a piece of lining fabric to cover it and glue in place. Place the cardboard piece in bottom of bag and remove when laundering.

OVAL CHART

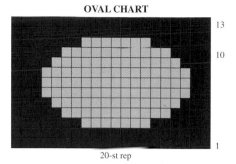

20-st rep

PAISLEY CHART

Color key

- ■ Grey (A)
- ■ Marigold (B)
- ■ Navy (C)
- ☐ Green (D)
- ☐ Couscous (E)
- ■ Raspberry (F)
- Ⅴ Duplicate stitch

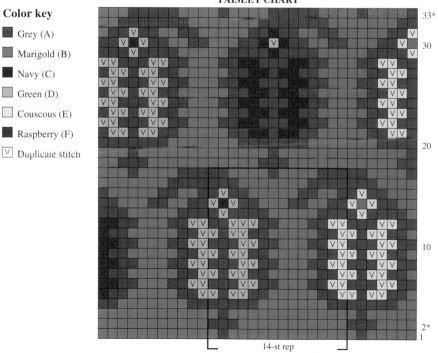

14-st rep

For Intermediate Knitters

Warm up to winter with pale frosted colors and snowflake and icicle patterning. Quick to knit on a circular needle, this cozy backpack has a drawstring top with color-tipped I-cord closure. Designed by Joan McGowan.

KNITTED MEASUREMENTS

■ Approx 15" x 12"/38cm x 30.5cm

MATERIALS

■ 5 1¾oz/50g balls (each approx 109yd/100m) of DiVe/Lane Borgosesia *Christine Melange* (mohair/wool/acrylic ④) in #24102 blue (MC)

■ 2 balls in #1807 ivory (A)

■ 1 ball in #1810 green (B)

■ Size 8 (5mm) circular needle, 16"/40cm long

■ 1 set (4) size 6 (4mm) dpn

■ ½yd/.5m of lightweight cotton canvas fabric for lining

■ Matching sewing threads

GAUGE

20 sts and 22 rnds to 4"/10cm over St st foll charts using size 8 (5mm) needle.
Take time to check gauge.

BODY

With circular needle and MC, cast on 128 sts. Join, taking care not to twist sts on needles. Mark end of rnd and sl marker every rnd. Work in St st for 3 rnds.

Beg charts

Foll chart 1, rep rnds 1 and 2 for 13 rnds. Foll chart 2, work rnds 1-13. Foll chart 3, work rnds 1-14. K 1 rnd with MC. Foll chart 4, work rnds 1-7 as foll: k1 MC,

work 6-st rep 21 times, k1 MC. K 1 rnd with MC. Foll chart 5, work rnds 1-15. K 2 rnds with MC. Foll chart 1, rep rnds 1 and 2 for 6 rnds.

Next (eyelet) rnd *K8, k2tog, yo; rep from *, end k8. With MC, k 8 rnds. Bind off.

BOTTOM OF BAG

With circular needle and MC, cast on 32 sts. Working back and forth in rows, work in St st for 50 rows. Bind off.

STRAPS

(make 2)
With dpn, cast on 22 sts. Divide sts on 3 needles. Work in rnds of St st for 27"/69cm. Bind off.

FINISHING

Block pieces to measurements.

LINING

Cut lining material using bottom of bag as a pattern adding ½"/1.25cm seam allowance on all sides. Cut lining for circular body to measure 23" x 14"/58cm x 35.5cm (with seam allowance on all edges). Sew back seam for 14"/35.5cm. Fit bottom lining to body and sew in place. Tack lining at top of bag under eyelet row. Using a sewing machine, sew 2 straps side by side at top at beg of chart 1. Sew lower edge of straps to lower part of bag at beg of chart 1 and leaving 1"/2.5cm free between straps. Reinforce stitching by sewing again.

I-cord

With B and 2 dpn, cast on 4 sts.

***Next row (RS)** K4, do not turn. Slide sts to beg of needle to work next row from

RS; rep from * until I-cord measures 1½"/4cm. Change to A and cont to work I-cord for 17"/43cm more. Then work with B for 1½"/4cm. Bind off. Pull I-cord through eyelet row.

Color key

■ Blue (MC)

☐ Ivory (A)

■ Green (B)

CHART 3

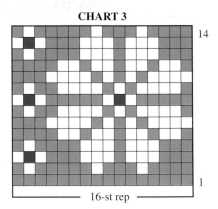

14

1

16-st rep

CHART 1

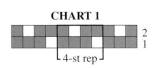

2
1

4-st rep

CHART 4

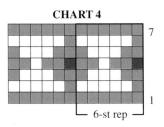

7

1

6-st rep

CHART 2

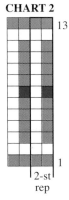

13

1

2-st rep

CHART 5

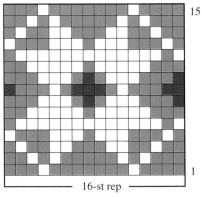

15

1

16-st rep

WOVEN-TEXTURED BAG
Basket case

Basketweave stitch adds textural interest to a clever handbag knit in the round. The extended circular handle is grafted invisibly at the center and the contrast-patterned flap is decorated with a crocheted tassel. Designed by Gitta Schrade.

KNITTED MEASUREMENTS

▓ Approx 12" x 16½"/30.5cm x 42cm (without strap)

MATERIALS

▓ 8 1¾oz/50g balls (each approx 106m/116yds) of Naturally/S.R. Kertzer *Cotton Candy DK* (cotton/wool ⑤) in #505 liquorice (MC),

▓ 1 ball in #506 jube (CC)

▓ Size 6 (4mm) circular needle, 32"/80cm long *or size to obtain gauge*

▓ One pair size 6 (4mm) needles

▓ One circular needle size 4 (3.5mm), 16"/40cm long, or set of dpns

▓ Crochet hook E/4 (3.5mm)

▓ Stitch holder

GAUGE

25 sts and 52 rows to 4"/10cm over basket st using size 6 (4mm) needles.

Take time to check gauge.

BASKET STITCH (IN RNDS)

(multiple of 10 sts)

Rnds 1 and 2 (RS) Knit.

Rnds 3-6 *P6, sl 4 wyib; rep from * around.

Rnds 7 and 8 Knit.

Rnds 9-12 P1, *sl 4 wyib, p6; rep from * to last 9 sts, sl 4 wyib, p5.

Rep rnds 1-12 for basket st in rnds.

BASKET STITCH (IN ROWS)

(multiple of 10 sts)

Row 1 (RS) Knit.

Row 2 Purl.

Rows 3 and 5 *P6, sl 4 wyib; rep from * to last 10 sts, p6, sl 2 wyib, k2.

Rows 4 and 6 P2, sl 2 wyif, k6, *sl 4 wyif, k6; rep from * to end.

Row 7 Knit.

Row 8 Purl.

Rows 9 and 11 P1, *sl 4 wyib, p6; rep from * to last 9 sts, sl 4 wyib, p5.

Rows 10 and 12 K5, sl 4 wyif; *k6, sl 4 wyif; rep from * to last st, k1.

Rep rows 1-12 for basket st in rows.

NOTE When shaping in pat, do not sl sts at beg or end of rows, but work these sts in St st.

PURSE

BODY

With size 6 (4mm) circular needle and MC, cast on 210 sts. Join, taking care not to twist sts on needle. Mark end of rnd and sl marker every rnd.

Work in rnds of basket st until piece measures 11"/28cm from beg, end with a WS row.

Divide and shape for strap

Next row (RS) Cont to work in rows of basket st, work 58 sts, turn, bind off next 11 sts for center front, work 47 sts (to end of rnd marker), do not turn, work 58 sts past marker, turn, cont to work on these sts only, bind off 11 sts for center back, leaving rem 94 sts on spare needle.

Next row (WS) Work across row 94 sts,

remove marker from center of row.
Keeping in pat, bind off 5 sts at beg of next 4 rows, 2 sts at beg of next 2 rows—70 sts. Dec 1 st at beg of next 52 rows—18 sts. Work even in pat for 9½"/24cm more, end with a row 1 or 7. Leave sts on holder.

With RS facing, rejoin yarn to rem 94 sts. Keeping in pat, bind off 5 sts at beg of next 4 rows, 2 sts at beg of next 2 rows—70 sts. Dec 1 st at beg of next 52 rows—18 sts. Work even in pat for 9½"/24cm more, end with a row 6 or 12. Graft strap sts tog knitwise.

FINISHING

With RS facing, crochet hook and MC, sl st around entire opening edge, beg at center front. Work 1 rnd sc around entire opening, using sl sts as base. Rep for back.

Flap

With size 6 (4mm) needles and MC, cast on 43 sts.

Row 1 (RS) P3, *k1-yo-k1 into next st, p3; rep from * to end.

Row 2 K3, *p3, k3; rep from * to end.

Row 3 P3, *k3, p3; rep from * to end.

Row 4 K3, *p3tog, k3; rep from * to end.

Row 5 Purl.

Row 6 Knit.

Row 7 P1, *k1-yo-k1 into next st, p3; rep from * to last 2 sts, k1-yo-k1 into next st, p1.

Row 8 K1, p3, *k3, p3; rep from * to last st, k1.

Row 9 P1, *k3, p3; rep from * to last 4 sts, k3, p1.

Row 10 K1, p3tog, *k3, p3tog; rep from * to last st, k1.

Row 11 Purl.

Row 12 Knit.

Rep rows 1-12 three times more.

Shape flap

Keeping in pat, dec 1 st at beg of next 8 rows, then dec 1 st each side of next 6 rows.

Next 2 rows Bind off 2 sts, work to last 2 sts, dec 1 st twice.

Next 2 rows Bind off 5 sts, work to last 2 sts, dec 1 st twice. Bind off rem 5 sts.

Edging

With RS of flap facing, smaller circular needle and CC, pick up and k 150 sts around entire flap, join. P 6 rnds, inc 1 st in each corner in first rnd then every other rnd. Bind off loosely. Sew edging to WS.

Tassel

With crochet hook and CC, ch 56, turn, sl st back. Fasten off. Make a 2nd cord in same way. With crochet hook and CC, ch 48, turn, sl st back. Fasten off. Make a 2nd cord in same way. Fold these 4 chains in half and secure ¾"/2cm down from top. Attach to flap. Sew flap to center back of purse, 1½"/4cm down from crochet edge.

BAA BAA BACKPACK

Have you any wool?

For Experienced Knitters

Cute and cuddly lamb will be loved by the young and the young at heart! Contrasting bouclé highlights the fun fleece, stuffing and embroidery creates the charming dimensional details. Designed by Jacqueline Van Dillen.

KNITTED MEASUREMENTS

■ Approx 11" /28cm square

MATERIALS

■ 6 1¾oz/50g balls (each approx 216yd/200m) of Brown Sheep *Fantasy Lace* (wool ④) in #110 beige (MC)

■ 1 4oz/113g balls (each approx 190yd/173m) of *Lamb's Pride Worsted* (wool ④) each in #M08 brown (A) and M76 grey (B)

■ Small amount of dark scrap yarn for face and limb details

■ One pair size 10 (6mm) needles *or size to obtain gauge*

■ Size 10 (6mm) circular needle, 16"/40cm long

■ Stitch holder

■ 14"/35.5cm zipper

■ 1yd/1m brown webbing ¾"/2cm wide

■ Two parachute clasps (to fit webbing)

■ Stuffing

■ ½yd/.5m scrap fabric for lining (optional)

GAUGES

■ 12 sts and 26 rows to 4"/10cm with 2 strands MC over garter st using size 10 (6mm) needles.

■ 13 sts and 19 rows to 4"/10cm with 2 strands A or B over St st using size 10 (6mm) needles.

Take time to check gauges.

NOTE

Work with 2 strands of a color held tog throughout.

BODY

(make 2 pieces)

With 2 strands MC, cast on 24 sts. Work in garter st, inc 1 st each side every 6th row 6 times—36 sts. Work even until piece measures 6"/15cm (or 40 rows) from beg, pm. Dec 1 st each side every 3rd row 12 times. Work even until 6"/15cm (or 40 rows) above marker. Bind off rem 12 sts.

ZIPPER BAND

With RS facing and 2 strands A, pick up and k 52 sts along top of body (above markers). Work in St st for 6 rows. Bind off.

GUSSET

With 2 strands MC, cast on 9 sts. Work in garter st for 148 rows. Place sts on a holder.

FEET

(make 2)

With 2 strands A, cast on 24 sts. Work in St st, inc 1 st each side every 4th row 3 times—30 sts. Bind off 9 sts at beg of next 2 rows. Work even on rem 12 sts for 12 rows. Bind off 2 sts at beg of next 4 rows. Bind off rem 4 sts.

LEGS

(make 2)

With 2 strands MC, cast on 18 sts. Work in garter st for 20 rows. Change to 2 strands A and work in St st for 12 rows.

Dec row (RS) Dec 1 st, k6, dec 1 st, k6, dec 1 st—15 sts. Cont in this way to dec 1 st each end and in center (3 sts dec'd in row) *every* row 3 times more. Bind off rem 6 sts.

FACE

With 2 strands B, cast on 16 sts. Work in St st for 6 rows. Dec 1 st each side on next row. Work 3 rows even. Dec 1 st each side on next row—12 sts. Work 5 rows even.
Next row (RS) K5, k2tog, k5—11 sts. Work 1 row even.
Next row K4, k3tog, k4—9 sts. Work 1 row even.
Next row K3, k3tog, k3—7 sts. Work 1 row even.
Next row K2, k3tog, k2—5 sts. Work 1 row even.
Next row K1, k3tog, k1—3 sts. Work 1 row even. Bind off.

HEAD

With RS facing, circular needle and 2 strands MC, pick up and k 84 sts evenly around outside edge of face. Join and work in rnds of garter st (p 1 rnd, k 1 rnd) for 8 rnds. Bind off.

EARS

(make 2)
With 2 strands B, cast on 8 sts. Work in St st for 12 rows.
Next row [K2tog] 4 times—4 sts.
Next row [P2tog] twice—2 sts. K2tog and fasten off last st.

FINISHING

Cutting lining (optional)
Using front, back, zipper bands and gusset pieces as a guide, cut lining pieces ½"/1.5cm larger.

Backpack straps
Cut two 4"/10cm lengths of webbing. Fold the lengths in half and slide bottom of parachute clasp on each one. Baste to lower edge of back body approx 6"/15cm apart. Cut two equal lengths of webbing to desired length. Attach top half of clasp to one end of each one and baste other end to top of back piece, approx 2"/5cm apart.

Cut a 4"/10cm length of webbing and fold in half. Baste to center back zipper band. Sew in zipper between zipper bands, encasing folded webbing in back seam for loop. Sew end of gusset to sides of zipper bands, then sew sides to lower edge of both body pieces to join front and back, catching webbing in seams.

Assembly

Sew center back seam of foot, fold flap and sew in place. Rep for other foot. Stuff feet and sew to lower edge of front body. With scrap yarn, work straight st in center of foot to form hoof (see photo).
Lightly stuff legs and sew to top of front body. Work straight sts with scrap yarn for hooves as before.
Embroider mouth, nose and eyes with scrap yarn (see photo). Stuff head and sew to front body. Attach ears to each side of head.

Lining

Assemble lining as for knitted pieces. With wrong sides facing, slip stitch inside bag along zipper edge.

NOTES

RESOURCES

US RESOURCES

Write to the companies listed below for purchasing and mail-order information.

AURORA YARNS
PO Box 3068
Moss Beach, CA 94038-3068

BAABAJOES WOOL COMPANY
PO Box 260604
Lakewood, CO 80226

BARUFFA
distributed by
Lane Borgosesia

BERROCO, INC.
PO Box 367
Uxbridge, MA 01569

BERNAT®
distributed by
Patons®

BLUE SKY ALPACAS
PO Box 387
St Francis, MN 55070

BROWN SHEEP CO., INC.
100662 County Road 16
Mitchell, NE 69357

CHERRY TREE HILL YARN
PO Box 254
East Montpelier, VT 05651

CLASSIC ELITE YARNS
300A Jackson Ave.
Lowell, MA 01852

CLECKHEATON
distributed by
Plymouth Yarn

CREATIVE FIBERS
5416 Penn Ave. S.
Minneapolis, MN 55419

DALE OF NORWAY, INC.
N16 W23390 Stoneridge Dr.
Suite A
Waukesha, WI 53188

DIVÉ
distributed by
Lane Borgosesia

FILATURA DI CROSA
distributed by
Tahki•Stacy Charles, Inc.

GARNSTUDIO
distributed by
Aurora Yarns

JCA
35 Scales Lane
Townsend, MA 01469

JUDI & CO.
18 Gallatin Drive
Dix Hills, NY 11746

K1C2, LLC
2220 Eastman Ave. #105
Ventura, CA 93003

LANE BORGOSESIA
PO Box 217
Colorado Springs, CO 80903

LANG
distributed by
Berroco, Inc.

LION BRAND YARN CO.
34 West 15th Street
New York, NY 10011

MISSION FALLS
distributed by
Unique Kolours

NATURALLY
distributed
S. R. Kertzer, Ltd.

PATONS®
PO Box 40
Listowel, ON N4W 3H3
Canada

PLYMOUTH YARN
PO Box 28
Bristol, PA 19007

REYNOLDS
distributed by
JCA

ROWAN
distributed by
Westminster Fibers

S. R. KERTZER, LTD.
105A Winges Road
Woodbridge, ON L4L 6C2
Canada

SKACEL COLLECTION, INC.
PO Box 88110
Seattle, WA 98138

TAHKI•STACY CHARLES, INC.
1059 Manhattan Ave.
Brooklyn, NY 11222

TAHKI YARNS
distributed by
Tahki•Stacy Charles, Inc.

TRENDSETTER YARNS
16742 Stagg Street
Suite 104
Van Nuys, CA 91406

UNIQUE KOLOURS
1428 Oak Lane
Downingtown, PA 19335

WESTMINSTER FIBERS
5 Northern Blvd.
Amherst, NH 03031

CANADIAN RESOURCES

Write to US resources for mail-order availability of yarns not listed.

AURORA YARNS
PO Box 228553
Aurora, ON L4G 6S6

BERNAT®
320 Livingstone Ave. S
Listowel, ON N4W 3H3

BERROCO, INC.
distributed by
R. Stein Yarn Corp.

CLASSIC ELITE YARNS
distributed by
S. R. Kertzer, Ltd.

CLECKHEATON
distributed by
Diamond Yarn

DIAMOND YARN
9697 St. Laurent
Montreal, PQ H3L 2N1
and
155 Martin Ross, Unit #3
Toronto, ON M3J 2L9

FILATURA DI CROSA
distributed by
Diamond Yarn

GARNSTUDIO
distributed by
Aurora Yarns

LANG
distributed by
R. Stein Yarn Corp.

MISSION FALLS
PO Box 224
Consecon, ON K0K 1T0

NATURALLY
distributed by
S. R. Kertzer, Ltd.

PATONS®
320 Livingstone Ave. S
Listowel, ON N4W 3H3

R. STEIN YARN CORP.
5800 St Denis
Suite 303
Montreal, PQ H2S 3L5

ROWAN
distributed by
Diamond Yarn

S. R. KERTZER, LTD.
105A Winges Rd.
Woodbridge, ON L4L 6C2

UK RESOURCES

Not all yarns used in this book are available in the UK. For yarns not available, make a comparable substitute or contact the US manufacturer for purchasing and mail-order information.

COATS CRAFTS UK
distributors of Patons®
PO Box 22
The Lingfield Estate
Darlington
Co Durham DL1 1YQ
Tel: 01325-365457

ROWAN YARNS
Green Lane Mill
Holmfirth
West Yorks HD7 1RW
Tel: 01484-681881

SILKSTONE
12 Market Place
Cockermouth
Cumbria, CA13 9NQ
Tel: 01900-821052

VOGUE KNITTING BAGS & BACKPACKS

Editor-in-Chief
TRISHA MALCOLM

Art Director
CHRISTINE LIPERT

Senior Editor
CARLA S. SCOTT

Managing Editor
DARYL BROWER

Instruction Writer
MARI LYNN PATRICK

Technical Illustration Editor/
Page Layout
LILA CHIN
CHI LING MOY

Knitting Coordinator
JEAN GUIRGUIS

Yarn Coordinator
VERONICA MANNO

Instructions Coordinator
CHARLOTTE PARRY

Editorial Coordinators
KATHLEEN KELLY
ELLEN LESPERANCE

Photography
BRIAN KRAUS, NYC
JUAN RÍOS
Photographed at Butterick Studios

Stylists
JANICE FERRO
MONICA GAIGE-ROSENSWEIG

Project Director
CAROLINE POLITI

Production Managers
LILLIAN ESPOSITO
WINNIE HINISH

Publishing Consultant
MIKE SHATZKIN, THE IDEALOGICAL COMPANY

President and CEO, Butterick® Company, Inc
JAY H. STEIN

Executive Vice President and Publisher, Butterick® Company, Inc
ART JOINNIDES